Contemporary English

Teacher's Book
for Pupils' Books 1 and 2

R Rossner P Shaw J Shepherd J Taylor P Davies

M

First published 1979

Published by
THE MACMILLAN PRESS LIMITED
London and Basingstoke
Companies and representatives throughout the world

ISBN 0 333 27367 2

Printed in UK by the Blackmore Press,
Longmead, Shaftesbury, Dorset.

ACKNOWLEDGMENT

The authors of *Contemporary English* wish to express
their gratitude to all the teachers and administrators who
made the piloting of the course possible and passed on
valuable suggestions, many of which are included in this
published edition. The authors would especially like to
thank Bertha Cea, Amelia Hansen, Thérèse De Vet, Nancy
Gonzalez, Walter Plumb and Gloria Torrano, without whose
help the thorough piloting of *Contemporary English* would
have been impossible.

Contents

List of language items in Pupil's Book 1

Unit	Verb Phrase	Noun Phrase	Prepositional Phrase	Sentence
ONE	is; isn't (is not)	a; an; the; it that; this singular nouns numerals	on; in; near; of	What. . . . .? Where . . . . ? Is . . . . .?
TWO	are; aren't	they plurals		Are . . . . .? and
THREE	can (permission)	very adjectives (colours) (nationality words) he; she article + profession	with; from	be + N + adj? How old. . . . .? What colour . . . . .? Who . . . . .?

FIRST REVIEW AND COMPLEMENTATION UNIT   I; you; we; these; those

Unit	Verb Phrase	Noun Phrase	Prepositional Phrase	Sentence
FOUR	am	her; his; my; your (poss.adj.) I; you (months)	under	so What . . . . . like?
FIVE	present progressive	her; him; them; us postmodification with prep. phrase	to at (the moment)	What . . . . doing?
SIX	can; can't (ability)	the time	past; to	What time . . . . .? How? but

SECOND REVIEW AND COMPLEMENTATION UNIT   our; their; possessive pronouns

Unit	Verb Phrase	Noun Phrase	Prepositional Phrase	Sentence
SEVEN	present simple (3rd person singular)		at (time) by (transport)	then Does . . . . .?
EIGHT	present simple (other persons)			Do . . . . .? How much . . . . .? (price)
NINE	has; have never once/twice a week, etc.	no (as det.) each		How much . . . . .? (quantity) How many . . . . .? How often . . . . .?

TEN	stative verbs	another	on (day)
	present simple	other	in (part of day)
	with frequency		in (season)
	words		after; before

List of language items in Pupil's Book 2

Unit	Verb Phrase	Noun Phrase	Prepositional Phrase	Sentence
ONE	present simple	some partitives (containers)		**There is** **There are**
TWO	present simple can, can't present progressive	**Some** a (an) **any** **countable and uncountable nouns** weight and measure	before after	There is There are **How much?** **How many?** Why not? Because. .
THREE	**Difference in use between present simple and present progressive**			questions with present simple and present continuous
FIRST REVIEW AND COMPLEMENTATION UNIT				
FOUR	**Has/have to** **want to** **like to** other verbs followed by 'to' + infinitive			**Why? Because . . .?** **Is there/are there?** **How much/many?**
FIVE		**possessive form of nouns (singular and plural)** possessive pronouns		**Whose**
SIX	present progressive present simple	possessive form	**Across, along, through, past, under, over, up, down, beside.** **between** revision of propositions of time, position and direction	there is/are whose

SECOND REVIEW AND COMPLEMENTATION UNIT

SEVEN	Was, were		complementation after 'be' there was, there were . . . short answers with was, were
EIGHT	past simple of irregular and regular verbs (affirmative)	for (time)	ago what happened!
NINE	past simple, interrogative and negative		short answers with 'did' Why . . . ? To + infinitive (purpose)
TEN	going to (future), (aff. neg. interrog.) past tense, present progressive	ordinals	which?

General outline and basic assumptions

General Outline

'Contemporary English' is a course in general English for adult and adolescent students. The series, which will consist of six books, takes the learner from the beginner stage to an intermediate level. Each book is accompanied by Teacher's Notes, (one Teacher's Book for each two Pupils' Books) taped material and a set of wallcharts.

Basic Assumptions

The authors have written 'Contemporary English' with some basic assumptions in mind. The first is that adult students, just like their younger counterparts need motivation, and to be interested in learning. This interest will come not so much from the fact of learning and using a language (most people spend a large part of their lives doing this) but from what they are using the language *for*. For this reason the authors have provided a wide range of different language activities (many of them involving problem-solving) focussed on information that is of itself interesting and varied. Thus it is hoped that instead of practising English merely for the sake of English, students will become sufficiently involved in *what* they are saying, the information they are asking for or supplying, to lose some of their self-consciousness and anxiety about *how* they are saying it. Of course, this does not mean that only the message is important, but rather that the complexities of English phonology, grammar and semantics and all the socio-cultural variables surrounding language are perhaps better approached indirectly, at least in the beginning. Students should have something to say before they are asked to talk, and what they have to say should be as varied and interesting to them as possible.

Secondly the authors have assumed that learning a foreign language is a complex and little understood process. What is clear is that the learner needs plenty of exposure and plenty of opportunity for activating what he has observed using the group of language skills he has already mastered in his own language. Thus, students are exposed to new language items some time before they need to use them (in reading passages for example), and quite a gap is allowed for between what a student can understand and what he can actually use himself. Moreover, it has been assumed that different students probably learn things in different ways, and so plenty of varied opportunities for cumulative and revision practice are provided methodically and regularly.

Finally the authors have assumed that the popular division of language syllabuses into structural and functional is not particularly helpful for the student, whose real problem is to learn how to use a body of language for effective communication of various kinds. Thus the syllabus on which 'Contemporary English' is based is 'multidimensional' in nature suggesting treatment of structures, lexis and functions of language hand in hand. In early books this allows students to make quick advances in useful language for everyday interaction whilst dealing at the same time with carefully graded structures and lexis. In later books the various dimensions of language will be fused as the student is gradually exposed to a wider range of use.

Activity types and handling notes

Teachers of English as a foreign and second language regularly use a wide variety of techniques in their work, and 'Contemporary English' may be successfully used in a number of different ways. However, the authors recommend consideration of certain well-tried techniques for the handling of the various activities offered in this series. The activities are listed here together with some handling notes on each. Every activity is given a letter which will be used wherever that activity occurs, throughout the Teacher's Book.

A **Listen and put a circle round the appropriate letter/word . . . . .**

This is usually found at the beginning of a teaching unit after the formulation of information. Its purpose is to ensure:

a that the student is exposed to new linguistic forms before practising them

b that he becomes familiar with the body of data he is to work with before starting practice.

For the activity to fulfil its purpose, everyone in the class should understand how the formulation works and how to obtain information from it. In some groups, prior study of the information may be helpful.

Each of the sentences to be listened to should be read clearly, at near normal speed. Students should be given sufficient time to deal with the information involved and to circle the appropriate letter. The excercise may be checked by asking individual students to give their answers, and listing the correct responses on the board.

B **Listen and complete the . . . . .**

This activity follows the major formulation in a unit where this has been left imcomplete; students are asked to show their understanding by filling in the information omitted. Students will need to see how the formulation works, and to be aware of the gaps, before beginning the activity. Answers are best written in pencil to allow for correction, since the information will be used later in oral and written exercises.

C Give information about . . . . .

Here students are asked to produce declaratives based on the data given. Structural control is tight, giving opportunities for drilling; the amount of information available allows for a wide range of different, though structurally similar, sentences to be produced.

As there is normally new language in these declaratives, teachers may wish to do some prior pronunciation drilling, and will certainly wish to clear up students' doubts about meaning, using an appropriate presentation technique (drawing, exemplification, mime, explanation, translation, etc.).

A degree of problem-solving is generally present, and it is hoped that students' conscious involvement will be with the content to be communicated rather than the language to be used. Teachers should overtly encourage this by allowing time for thought before answers are required, and even stimulating modest 'research' by the students. Use of enlargements of the formulations in the classroom helps to focus students' attention on content (and allows books to be closed). However, the teacher should not lose sight of the central issue — the learning of the form and use of English.

D Ask for or supply information about . . . . .

These 'question-and-answer' exercises often involve the activation of new question forms; this will require drilling, and particular attention to stress and intonation. However, this should be seen as a preliminary stage to interaction of a more communicative kind, which can be enhanced by preventing half the students from having access to the information needed to answer questions that arise. Pair work and group work are particularly rewarding with this activity, once the new structures involved have been clearly established with the class as a whole. Again, attention should be paid to appropriacy of questions and responses, as well as linguistic accuracy.

Out of this activity, opportunities usually arise for similar practice making use of local or personal information supplied by the students themselves. This information naturally varies from one class to another; the Teacher's Book contains suggestions for possible approaches, which should be followed up according to local circumstances.

E Read the following sentences and complete them . . . . .
This activity links practice of the written form to the preceding oral activities; such association clarifies and reinforces.

In some cases, teachers will find it useful to prepare these exercises orally with their students.

Teachers may prefer students to write this kind of exercise out in full in their notebooks. Model completions are provided in the Teacher's Notes.

F Act out the dialogue . . . . .
Frame dialogues, usually with possible alternatives supplied, are seen as an important cumulative practice activity. They also offer opportunities to practise stress and intonation, and to increase the students' range of conversational expressions. After some initial drilling of the base dialogue, students should be encouraged to act out the dialogues in groups or in front of the class. Where the alternatives are complex, some time may be needed to follow the sequence through.

G The Reading Comprehension Section
These sections fulfil a dual purpose:
a they develop the students' ability to extract information from texts written at a linguistic level significantly above their productive capacity
b they expose students to linguistic items which they will shortly be required to handle actively.

In pursuit of point (a), the questions precede the passage, in order to direct the students' search for specific information. This focuses attention on what students *can* extract from the passage rather than on the difficulties they encounter. A short time limit should be set, and the teacher should not deal with students' questions until after the exercise has been attempted. After checking answers (provided in the Teacher's Notes), the vocabulary, topic dealt with, etc. may be discussed if students so desire. However, in this regard it should be remembered that vocabulary is more wide ranging and less controlled than in the body of the units, and that such discussion is *not* the primary purpose of these passages.

Later in the series, activities related to cohesive elements in the passages are introduced.

H The Interaction Sequences

Though they may be handled like the dialogues, the interaction sequences are different from the dialogues in a number of ways. First, they are organised *functionally,* i.e. according to what the speakers are trying to achieve. Second, structural control is not, here, the base; structures which appear desirable for the realization of the function are included. Third, there is no cumulative intention in relation to the language used, though the functions are loosely sequenced, and more complex manifestations of a function frequently appear at a later stage.

It is important to note that throughout the book all the language is intended to be authentic, but the interaction sequences supply a separate stream of language for realizing functions which would not fit comfortably into a course based only on syntactic control. Most of the sequences will be found useful as a part of classroom language. Where students hear English outside the classroom setting these sequences will acquire more importance, and students should be encouraged to use combinations of different sequences as frequently as possible.

I The Grammar Summaries

These summaries are intended to be directly informative. Students should be shown how they work, and encouraged to use them to consciously confirm and reinforce the syntactic data they have already received situationally. It is not necessary to analyse them with students, unless a need to do so becomes evident.

J The Review and Complementation Units

These appear at regular intervals throughout the course. The exercises they contain are varied in type, but share a primary concern with form rather than function. Since they normally offer the seventh* different way in which the student encounters a particular language item in the course, these exercises may be seen as rounding off, or testing, the students' knowledge of the points involved.

These units occasionally contain linguistic items that have previously only been introduced in the Teacher's Book though they complement what has been taught in the body of the course.

* The others, in order of appearance: receptively, in reading passages and listening comprehension; productively, in the activation of the oral and written forms; in the grammar summaries, and in cumulative practice exercises.

Note on contractions
Contractions are seen as characteristic of the spoken rather than the written mode; consequently, where language in the book is intended for oral/aural use, contractions are generally used; elsewhere, the full form appears.

Pair work and group work
Many of the activities in 'Contemporary English' lend themselves to pair or group work. This provides opportunities for students to practise in a more typical interaction configuration (they communicate with one, two or three people instead of with the whole group), and therefore to learn from and help each other more directly. The amount of oral practice each student engages in is thereby greatly increased, and further variety is added to classroom activities.

Pair work may involve oral, written, reading or even listening activities. In every case, however, the ground must be carefully prepared beforehand, as students will have to work together without close supervision. Thus it is necessary to introduce and demonstrate the activity before the students embark upon it. During such work, the teacher will wish to circulate in search of individual student difficulties. These activities should never last more than five or ten minutes at a stretch, and groups or partners should be changed regularly.

Creating an 'information gap'
(These suggestions are for those teachers who have the resources at their disposal to produce simple visual aids and wish to make student-student interaction in the classroom more realistic (and more interesting) than is possible when all or half the students are looking at a body of information in their books.)

1   It is clearly preferable for students to raise their eyes from their books and look at some focal point and each other. There are wallcharts available with each Pupil's Book for this purpose.

2 Some teachers may wish to try the 'split group' approach. In this case two complementary wallcharts will be needed. Each will have the same framework, but only half the necessary information. For example, the airport timetable from Unit Seven can be left incomplete: one of the wallcharts would contain, three destination cities, two 'via' cities, three departure times and two arrival times, while the other would contain the remaining information. Once the wallcharts have been made, the only remaining problem is to divide the class into two groups facing each other across the classroom and to suspend or place the wallcharts back to back between the two groups (an easel will be useful here). Students can then ask and answer 'genuine' questions to which only people in the other group have the answer.

3 A similar sort of visual aid can be produced for group or pair work. In this case sets of small complementary visual aids will be needed for distribution round the class. Incomplete sets of information can be reproduced on fairly small pieces of card (perhaps with a washable surface) or on mimeographed sheets. Students in pairs or groups would then ask and answer questions in order to fill in, at least mentally, the missing information.

Use of Taped Material

The tapes which accompany each Pupils' Book (available in cassette or open-reel) contain pronunciation models, listening and reading comprehension material, examples from some question-answer exercises, and all the dialogues and interaction sequences. All exercises for which there is material on tape are marked in the Teacher's Notes to each unit.

In general the material on tape provides teachers with an opportunity to expose their students to different voices in the classroom, and offers an interesting means of presenting role-playing type exercises.

A **The pronunciation models**, of which phonetic transcriptions are offered in the Teacher's Book, are for reference only. The pronunciation used is standard British, and the stress and intonation patterns used are, as far as possible in decontextualized examples, normal for standard British. The use of this style of pronunciation on the tapes *in no way* implies that standard British pronunciation is 'the best', or that it is the one teachers and students should use. It is simply widely understood and neutral, and therefore convenient for a tape.

B The listening comprehension material on tape allows the teacher to develop her/his students' ability to understand English without being able to see the speaker (as in a telephone conversation) – a more difficult skill than face to face talk. Teachers may need to press the 'pause' button after each sentence in order to allow students time to circle a letter, write, draw, etc. In some cases, it may be desirable to rewind and give students a second chance.

C The exercise examples are all taken from question-answer or role-playing exercises. They are designed to 'warm up' students and show them how the exercises relate to their subject matter. Having heard the examples, students should be able to continue asking and answering questions, or role-playing, themselves.

D The dialogues and interaction sequences are reproduced on tape to aid teachers in presentation. Teachers may ask students to close their books while they listen to the dialogue or interaction sequence once or twice. At the same time comprehension can be checked and vocabulary and pronunciation difficulties can be cleared up. Afterwards students may be asked to reproduce, adapt and act out the dialogue or sequence themselves.

Students who are particularly concerned to work on their own pronunciation may be invited to use the tapes in a listening centre or for home study.

E. Some teachers have found it useful to have these passages available on tape, both for subsequent use in the classroom (after the material has been used for its primary reading comprehension function) and for use in the language laboratory.

F A reference list of the proper names used in the text is provided for the convenience of teachers.

The Phonetic Symbols

VOWEL

1	iː	miː	me
2	i	it	it
3	e	get	get
4	æ	æt	at
5	ɑː	ɑː	are
6	ɔ	nɔt	not
7	ɔː	ɔːl	all
8	u	put	put
9	uː	duː	do
10	ʌ	ʌp	up
11	əː	həː	her
12	ə	ə'gou	ago

DIPHTHONG

13	ei	sei	say
14	ou	nou	no
15	ai	mai	my
16	au	nau	now
17	ɔi	bɔi	boy
18	iə	iə	ear
19	eə	eə	air
20	ɔə	ɔə	oar
21	uə	tuə	tour

CONSONANT

22	p*	pei	pay
23	b	biː	be
24	t*	tiː	tea
25	d	duː	do
26	k*	kɑː	car
27	g	gou	go
28	f*	fɑː	far
29	v	vein	vain
30	θ*	θin	thin
31	ð	ðis	this
32	s*	sou	so
33	z	iz	is
34	ʃ*	ʃip	ship
35	ʒ	'viʒn	vision
36	tʃ*	mʌtʃ	much
37	dʒ	eidʒ	age
38	h*	hiz	his
39	m	miː	me
40	n	nou	no
41	ŋ	siŋ	sing
42	r	red	red
43	l	lɑːst	last
44	w	wiː	we
45	j	juː	you

Detailed notes for Pupil's Book 1

Unit one

This first unit is designed to:
1 introduce some vocabulary items to serve as a basis for communicative practice
2 introduce the determiners 'a', 'an', and 'the'
3 introduce the numerals
4 introduce the pronouns 'it', 'this' and 'that'
5 get students to communicate efficiently about the identity and location of objects and famous places using 'what', 'where' and one or two prepositions
6 establish types of activity that will recur throughout *'Contemporary English'*

PRONUNCIATION MODELS

A postcard, please. /ə`pouskɑ:d `pli:z/
An apple, please. /ən `æpəl `pli:z/
Where's the calculator ? /weəz ðə `kælkjuleitə/
It's in the cupboard. / its in ðə `kʌbəd/
What's this ? /`wɒts `ðis/

Exercise one

(Introduction of a few items of vocabulary and distinction between 'a' and 'an')

Real objects or pictures of them may be used to 'present' the vocabulary. Teachers may wish to add to the list of words to suit their own needs and situations. The words suggested are designed to fit in with exercise 3 and its situation.

Although the authors have assumed that students will be absolute beginners, many adolescent and adult students will know the odd word of English. This fact should be exploited: individual students may be able to tell the class what the English is for a given item. However, each word will need to be carefully modelled by the teacher so that students have a fair opportunity to hear the word clearly before being asked to produce it.

After some (choral and individual) repetition drilling, the numbers in the book or the real objects at the teacher's disposal may be used as cues for quick cue-response practice, which should not be abandoned until all students can say the words confidently and accurately.

1

| **Exercise two** | (Checking of students' comprehension (aural) of the words |
| **(A)** | introduced) |

It will probably be necessary to practise the numbers 1 to 10 before doing this exercise.

The following are suggestions only:

(Point to drawings or pick up objects or picture cards.)

1 Point to a comb; say 'a comb'.
2 Point to an apple; say 'an orange'.
3 Point to a pen; say 'a lighter'.
4 Point to a cup of coffee; say 'a cup of coffee'.
5 Point to a postcard; say 'a postcard'.
6 Point to an orange; say 'a sandwich'.
7 Point to a lighter; say 'a lighter'.
8 Point to a pipe; say 'a pen'.

Note It should not be necessary and is not desirable to use 'it is' or 'it's'.

| **Exercise three** ⓣ | (Practice with the vocabulary in a realistic setting and |
| **(F)** | introduction of some useful phrases) |

Real objects will be very useful here. If group work is to be used, students can be asked to do their own drawings on small pieces of paper or to bring their own realia if desired. The alternatives for 'madam' are 'sir' or 'miss'.

Note The prices will only become useful in exercise 5.

| **Exercise four** | (Practice of the numbers 1 to 10) |
| **(4a)** | |

After some initial repetition drilling of these numbers or some sample telephone numbers, students should be able to produce numbers they know in English or read off invented numbers from the board, from advertisements, etc.

Note Phone numbers in English are always said digit by digit (except for 'double six' etc.) and zero is usually pronounced 'oh' /oʊ/ .

(4b) (Introduction and practice of the numbers 11 to 99)

After some initial repetition drilling, students can be asked to read a few famous dates and to mention dates (years) that are interesting to them. (These will derive mainly from world and local history).

| **Exercise five** ⓣ | (More practice of vocabulary and numerals in a realistic |
| **(F)** | setting) |

Students will need to do this activity while looking at the illustration that accompanies exercise 3, or an enlargement of it.

Note 'p' (pence) is pronounced like the letter p.

| **Exercise six** | (Introduction and practice of a new set of vocabulary and the determiner 'the')
This exercise should be approached in the same way as exercise 1. |
|---|---|

Exercise seven ⊤
(A)

(Exposure to the new form 'is' and the prepositions 'in' and 'on')
It is not necessary to present the new elements explicitly since students can do the exercise using their knowledge of vocabulary. The sentences, which are suggestions only, should be read at a fairly normal speed, twice each.

1	The calculator is on the desk.	NO
2	The apple is on the floor.	YES
3	The pen is on the desk.	NO
4	The coffee pot is in the cupboard.	NO
5	The telephone is on the desk.	NO
6	The calculator is in the cupboard.	YES
7	The calendear is in the drawer.	YES
8	The clock is on the floor.	NO
9	The calculator is on the shelf.	YES
10	The typewriter is on the floor.	NO

Exercise eight ⊤
(D)

(Introduction and practice of 'where' and 'it')
Drawings of these and similar objects distributed differently in the room can be used to extend this activity. It may be more interesting to cover the drawings after letting students study them for a while.
Note 'the' directly preceding a vowel is usually pronounced /ði/ e.g. /ði: æpəˌl/ the apple.
Some teachers may wish to introduce the question form 'Is the _____ on the _____ ?' and the answers 'Yes, it is.' and 'No, it isn't.' at this stage. This can be done using the same illustration after a short period of repetition drilling.

Exercise nine
(E)

(Writing practice of the same items)
The anticipated completions are as follows:

a desk	f pen _____ on
b floor	g The clock is
c calendar	h is the; floor
d calculator _____ on	i is the calendar
e calculator _____ in	j Where is the calculator

Exercise ten
(C)

(Introduction of a new vocabulary set and further practice of 'is', 'the' and 'a')
This activity can easily be extended by getting students to talk about their own locality or a town they know well.

(D)   (Introduction and practice of the 'yes/no' question form
                 and short answers)
                     This exercise can easily be extended to talk about real
                 places known to the students.

Exercise eleven ⓣ   (Realistic practice of 'where' and the prepositions as used
(F)   when asking for and giving directions; introduction of 'on
                 the right' and 'on the left' and 'near')
                     The new phrases 'on the right/left' are best presented in
                 the classroom. In practice with the plan provided, the
                 location of the people speaking is of great importance.
                 Once again the activity can be extended by getting
                 students to ask for and give directions to various places in
                 the vicinity of the classroom/institutution.

Exercise twelve   (Writing practice of the same items)
(E)   The anticipated completions are as follows:
                 a hotel; the _____ station
                 b restaurant; near _____ hospital
                 c left _____ Gardenia Restaurant
                 d is _____ left _____ cinema
                 e Is _____ cinema; it is
                 f is on the left _____ the Highway Motel

Exercise thirteen   (Presentation and practice of 'what' and 'this/that')
(D)   'This' and 'that' should be presented and practised in
                 the classroom before beginning exercise 13. This can be
                 done in many ways; one is to pass round real objects or
                 picture cards (preferably known vocabulary) and to get
                 students to make statements like 'This is a pipe' or 'That's
                 an apple' about what they and others are holding. By
                 ensuring that the objects are continually passed round and
                 by providing clear and rapid cues, the teacher will be able
                 to achieve considerable practice in a short period of time.
                     Postcards or drawings of the places suggested will
                 clearly be of great usefulness during this activity, and
                 students should be encouraged to bring along postcards
                 and pictures of famous tourist attractions that they know
                 (or do not know!) about.
                 Note Two distinct uses of the demonstratives are demon-
                 strated here: in 'What's this?' the pronoun is used
                 deictically i.e. to point out something in his range of
                 vision; in 'Where's that?', however, the pronoun is used
                 anaphorically i.e. to refer back to the previous exchange.
                 In this case, 'that' cannot be replaced by 'this'. (Although
                 as will be noted from the reading texts, 'this' is very often
                 used anaphorically in continuous explanatory discourse.)

| **Exercise fourteen** | (Writing practice with 'where', 'is', 'in', 'isn't', etc.) |
| **(E)** | The anticipated completions are as follows: |

a Where; is in   d What is; It is the

b Where is the; It is in   e Is ____ in; it is not

c Is the ____ in; it is

Exercise fifteen   (Reading comprehension)

(G)   This exercise is intended as an introduction for students to the kind of activity they will be asked to do in future reading comprehension sections. It should be possible for them to complete it very quickly.

Unit two

The second unit introduces the plural form of some nouns and several items related to the plural: the verb form 'are', the pronoun 'they', and questions that parallel those already introduced in Unit One such as 'What are . . . ?' and 'Where are . . . ?'. The new vocabulary sets are crockery and cutlery, and the words of direction/location 'north', 'south', etc.

PRONUNCIATION MODELS

They're forks. /ðeə `fɔːks/
Six plates are £5.10. /'siks 'pleits ə 'faiv 'paundz 'ten `piː/
Where are the glasses? /'waər ə ðə `glɑːsiz/
They're on the top shelf. /ðeər ɔn ðə 'top `ʃelf/

Exercise one

(Introduction of some plural forms and practice of 'They are . . . ')

This introductory exercise should be done quickly using real objects or cards to present the new vocabulary and clarify the distinction between singular and plural. It will be noted that the three most common kinds of plural ending are intentionally mixed. ('plates', 'forks' and 'cups' all end in /s/, 'knives' and 'spoons' in /z/ and 'glasses' in /iz/. The consonant change in 'knives' should also be noted.) Some teachers may wish to spend a little time on intensive pronunciation drilling of these forms and the plurals of nouns introduced in Unit One. The following lists may be of use:

Pipes, cups, clocks, coffee pots, desks, restaurants.
Lighters, postcards, combs, pens, apples, telephones, calendars, typewriters, chairs, cupboards, drawers, shelves, stations, hotels, motels, hospitals, cinemas.
Sandwiches, oranges, churches, post offices.

Exercise two
(C)

(Practice of the plural forms in contrast with singular forms and further practice of numbers)

After practice of simple examples, which can be read off the visual, students should be encouraged to use their initiative to produce more interesting examples, such as the third example in the exercise. Teachers may wish to allow their students thirty seconds or so in which to do the necessary mental arithmetic individually. Then it should be possible for practice to continue at a rapid pace with students volunteering the examples they have worked out.

Exercise three (E)

(Writing practice of plural forms, 'are' and 'they')
  The anticipated completions are as follows:
a cups and saucers   d One _____ is
b are; They are   e knives are
c Six _____ are

Exercise four (F)

(Practice of the plurals in a realistic context; introduction of the phrases: 'Is that all?' and 'Thanks')
  Once again, real objects will be very useful when students are acting out the dialogue in groups or at the front of the classroom. It will be advisable to mix singulars and plurals and to encourage students in groups to work out dialogues involving problem-solving (eight glasses, fourteen spoons, etc.).

Exercise five

(Presentation of top and bottom)
  This exercise need only take a minute: the meanings of the new words can be demonstrated using furniture, etc. in the classroom. Then the illustrations in the book can be used to clarify them.

Exercise six (C)

(Practice of the plurals and 'are' with the prepositions 'in' and 'on')
  This exercise provides students with another easy opportunity to work with the new plural forms and two of the prepositions from Unit One. Some teachers may wish to introduce 'aren't' at this point by getting students to contradict false statements:
Student 1   The glasses are in the cupboard.
Student 2   They aren't in the cupboard. They're on the top shelf.
Student 1   Oh, yes. Sorry.

Exercise seven (A) Ⓣ

(Aural comprehension practice involving plurals)
  The suggested sentences are:
1 The cups and saucers are on the bottom shelf.   T
2 The plates are in the cupboard.   T
3 The knives are in the bottom drawer.   F
4 The glasses are on the top shelf.   T
5 The spoons are in the cupboard.   F
6 The forks aren't in the top drawer.   F

7

7 The cups and saucers aren't on the top shelf.　　　T
8 The spoons are in the top drawer.　　　F

Exercise eight
(D)

(Oral practice of 'Where are . . . ?' and 'They are . . . ')
　　As with exercise 8 in Unit One, it may be more
interesting for some students if they are asked to
remember the location of the various items. This exercise,
too, can be extended by the use of objects in the
classroom or of alternative illustrations or drawings on the
board.
　　Further extension still can include the introduction of
'Are the . . . ?' and 'No, they aren't' so that students
practise a sequence of four utterances:
Student 1 Are the plates on the top shelf?
Student 2 No, they aren't.
Student 1 Where are they?
Student 2 In the cupboard.
Note Some teachers may prefer students to omit 'They
are' in their answers. (Where are the forks? In the top
drawer.)

Exercise nine
(E)

(Further writing practice for consolidation)
　　The anticipated completions are as follows:
a spoons　　　　　　　　　d are the glasses
b on the bottom shelf　　　e Where; In the top drawer
c are in the cupboard

Exercise ten ⓣ
(F)

(Further practice of plural forms and 'where' in a realistic
context; introduction of the items 'dear', 'O.K.' and 'Here
they are')
　　As this is the first dialogue of any real length, it is
important for students to realize that with a little
intensive drilling, they can easily memorize and act out a
dialogue accurately, and that, having done that, they can
easily adapt it as they wish.

Exercise eleven ⓣ
(A)

(Listening comprehension practice of plurals in contrast
with singular forms)
　　In this activity students are asked to discriminate
between plural forms and singular forms: thus it is
particularly important that the sentences are said at
normal speed with normal stress and weak forms.
　　The suggested sentences are:
(1—5 need not be related to any visual situation)
　　1 The fork's in the drawer.
　　2 The forks are in the drawer.
　　3 The apples are on the table.

4 The plate's in the cupboard.
5 The sandwiches are ten p.

(6–10 should relate to objects in the classroom, previously placed by the teacher)
6 The pen's on the table (desk).
7 The pens are on the floor.
8 The combs are in the drawer.
9 The lighter's on the desk (table).
10 The oranges are on the chair.

Exercise twelve
(E)

(Writing practice of mixed singular and plural pronouns and verb forms)
The anticipated completions are as follows:
is; it; is; are; they; are on; they, on; It

Exercise thirteen
(D)

(Further cumulative oral practice)
Most students will find the activity easier if they have an opportunity to practise saying the new names first. Later the exercise can be extended by encouraging students to talk about tourist attractions in the country where the class is being held.

Exercise fourteen
(C)

(Introduction and practice of 'north', 'south', etc.)
Some teachers may prefer to begin with practice about the country where the class is being held, or of some other country which is well known to students. A large map will be of great help.
Note As in many countries, regions in the USA are given names which do not necessarily correspond fully with the points of the compass.

Exercise fifteen
(D)

(Cumulative oral practice)
This exercise is in the form of a four-phrase exchange. It is important that one student should ask both questions and another student provide both answers. Although only one example is provided, the intention is that both singular and plural proper names be used.

Exercise sixteen
(E)

(Further writing practice involving singular and plural forms)
The anticipated completions are:
a Where is; it _____ in
b Where are; are in
c Is; it is not; in New Orleans
d Are _____ in; they are
e Where are; They are in New Mexico

Exercise seventeen

(Further oral and writing practice for consolidation)
This exercise should be done orally first. It provides opportunities for practising 'It is . . . ' and 'They are . . . '
The answers are as follows: ('It is in . . . ' or 'They are in . . . ')

a South America	f Russia
b Madrid	g Paris
c Rome	h Copenhagen
d London	i Rio de Janeiro
e Greece	j Venezuela

Reading comprehension (G)

This exercise can be done very quickly individually or in groups after the passage has been read silently.

Note Although Kosciusko is a real mountain, Caldong is a fictitious town.

The answers are as follows:

1 d	4 a	7 h
2 g	5 f	8 b
3 e	6 c	

Note For 'these' and 'those' see the First Review and Complementation Unit, page 15.

Unit three

The third unit is designed to introduce and provide
practice of the following important language elements:
the syntax and use of items concerned with description,
particularly certain adjectives, used attributively and
predicatively, and expressions of age and nationality; the
pronouns 'he' and 'she' (and also 'I' and 'you'); the new
question types 'How old . . . ?', 'What colour . . . ?',
'Who . . .?' and 'Can I have . . . ?' and the prepositions
'with' and 'from' in prepositional phrases of description.
(For 'I' and 'we' see the First Review and Complementation Unit, page 15)

PRONUNCIATON MODELS
The Concorde is fast. /ðə ˈkɔŋkɔːd iz ˋfɑːst/
Frank West is a tall man. /ˈfræŋk ˈwest iz əˋtɔːl ˌmæn/
He's a tall man with fair hair. /hiːz ə ˈtɔːl ˈmæn wið ˈfeə ˋheə/
How old is she? /ˈhau ˋould iz ʃiː/
What colour are they? /wɔt ˋkʌlər aː ðei/

Exercise one
(C)

(Introduction and oral practice of some adjectives used in
affirmative sentences)
  Before beginning this exercise, write the answers for line
1 of the chart on the board: very small, small, big, very big.
Also write clues for line 2: cheap, expensive; line 3: slow,
fast; line 4: uncomfortable, comfortable. Students should
be encouraged to work out the meaning of the new words
(adjectives) and to fill in the spaces in the chart. The
symbols should assist them with these tasks. After some
repetition drilling of the new words, practice can begin in
the normal way and include extension into cars known to
the students.

Exercise two ⓣ
(D)

(Oral practice of 'yes/no' questions involving adjectives)
  Many students will find the word order used in this kind
of question hard to adjust to. Some teachers may prefer
to practise the variant 'Is the Comet a comfortable car?'
in addition to the form suggested.

Exercise three (E)	(Writing practice for consolidation)

Exercise three
(E)

(Writing practice for consolidation)
   In this exercise students are asked to choose from a number of alternatives. However, (c) is limited to 'The Comet is an expensive car.'

Exercise four

(Reading comprehension)
   Students may be asked to work out the completions to the chart in groups. Although some of the vocabulary will be new, it is useful for students to use their powers of deduction and the little English they know to solve the problem (preferably in pencil first). Sections 4 and 5 can then be checked against the model provided by the teacher.

Exercise five ①
(A)

(Aural comprehension practice and familiarization with the information to be used in practice)
   Teachers may wish to allow students time to study the information provided in the chart before beginning exercise 5. This and a little guidance should enable them to see how the chart functions and relate the information with the pictures above. However, thorough presentation of new vocabulary should be left until after exercise 5 to allow students to work out as much as possible for themselves.
   The suggested sentences are:

1	Helen West is Scottish.	T
2	Frank West is a very young man.	F
3	Helen West is a tall woman with red hair.	T
4	Christopher West is a tall boy with black hair and blue eyes.	F
5	Nat Wilkins is 24 years old.	F
6	Madeleine is a very tall woman.	F
7	Frank West is a computer salesman.	T
8	Madeleine is from Paris.	T

Exercise six
(C)

(Oral practice of declarative sentences describing people's physical appearance)
   Although the example provided is in the affirmative, some teachers may wish to elicit negative sentences too (by contradiction, etc.). During this exercise all vocabulary should be clarified as it becomes necessary.

Exercise seven
(D)

(Introduction and oral practice of 'How old . . . ?')
   This exercise can easily be expanded by getting students to talk about famous living people, etc. In this case it will be helpful to introduce the word 'about . . .'.
   Note Teachers may prefer the simpler answer without 'years old'.

Exercise eight (C)	(Further cumulative practice of expressions of description)

Exercise eight
(C)

(Further cumulative practice of expressions of description)

    In this activity it is important that students begin to produce series of connected sentences rather than isolated sentences, and that they use pronouns as linking elements. This activity can also be expanded by encouraging students to talk about famous living people or members of their families. (In the latter case it will be necessary to introduce 'my' and one or two relationship words, 'brother', 'sister', etc.)

Exercise nine
(E)

(Writing practice of descriptive expressions)

    The anticipated completions are as follows:

a is	d are
b is a tall _____ grey	e is a
c is from; She is	f How old; is (+ a number)

Exercise ten

(Further practice in writing (communicative writing))

    Students will find the exercise easier to do if a complete model is built up on the board with their help first. After this has been studied and erased, students in pairs or groups can be asked to work out their own paragraphs about their own chosen celebrity (celebrities). This can then be read to the class and/or collected for checking. **Note** Some students may need help in choosing a celebrity.

Exercise eleven

(Transfer of information)

    Here students are asked to reverse the usual process by matching the information they have assembled to the pattern they worked with previously. This and the preceding exercise can be done at home if preferred. (This will allow students to carry out 'research' if necessary.)

Exercise twelve ⊤
(A)

(Practice in distinguishing between 'he' and 'she')

    In this exercise students are asked to listen to sentences (unrelated to information in the book) and decide whether the pronouns they hear are masculine or feminine.

    The suggested sentences are:

1 He's very tall.
2 He's from Paris.
3 Is she young?
4 She isn't a secretary.
5 How old is he?
6 She's English.

7 He's forty-five years old.

8 Where is she?

Note It is important to maintain normal speed and stress throughout. 'He' and 'she' are unstressed in these examples.

Exercise thirteen

(Introduction and practice of a new vocabulary group)

Picture cards should be used to make practice more stimulating if they are available. The exercise should take a minute or two only.

Exercise fourteen
(D)

(Introduction and oral practice with 'What colour . . . ?' and a few colour adjectives)

Since colours are not available in the textbook, the adjectives should be introduced with the aid of coloured picture cards or objects in the classroom.

Note This exercise also provides opportunities to consolidate the singular – plural distinction and 'What . . . ?'

Exercise fifteen ⓣ
(F)

(Further cumulative practice of expressions of description, introduction of 'Who . . .?' and the expressions 'Really?' 'Can I have . . . ?' and 'Of course')

The suggestions for variation provided can be assigned to the various pairs or groups in the class so that alternative versions can be worked out and rehearsed (after the 'model' dialogue has been mastered).

Interaction
sequence ⓣ
(H)

(Practice of 'Can I have . . . ?' as a means of requesting.)

Some teachers may wish to extend practice by setting up extra situations after practice in the classroom. Students can be told to imagine that they are in a restaurant, hotel, aeroplane, etc.

Reading
comprehension ⓣ
(G)

The answers are as follows:

1 F	4 T	7 F
2 T	5 F	8 T
3 F	6 T	

First review and complementation unit

As will be clear from the grammar presentation, at the beginning of the unit, certain items appearing in this unit have not been introduced or practised formally in previous exercises. The new items are the determiners/demonstrative pronouns 'these' and 'those' (though students practised with the pronouns 'this' and 'that' in Unit Two) and the personal pronouns 'I' and 'we' and the verb form 'am' (though many teachers will have introduced these outside the context of the activities in *'Contemporary English'*).

Below are one or two suggestions for introduction and practice of these items, which were felt to be ill-suited for the sort of treatment other items have been given in the first three units.

These/Those The use of these words as pronouns of 'pointing' (deixsis) can be practised along with the use of 'this' and 'that'. If objects or picture cards are passed among students, practice can take the following form:
Student 1 (pointing) What's that?
Student 2 (showing) It's a lighter.
Student 3 (showing) What are these?
Student 4 They're oranges. Etc.

The use of this group of words as deictic determiners can be practised along with colours:
Student 1 (showing) What colour's this book?
Student 2 It's red.
Student 3 (pointing) What colour are those plates?
Student 4 They're blue.

I/We There are many obvious ways of practising these pronouns: one that will follow on well from Unit Three, exercise 8 is as follows:
Student 1 Hans and I are students. We're German.
Hans   Yes. Helga is from Bremen and I am from Hamburg. We're 17 years old. Etc.

The following is a brief key to the exercises in the unit:

Exercise one

(Practice of the present tense of the verb 'to be' and subject pronouns)

Are; is; he; he, am; She; am; you; is _____ is; they; are; It

Exercise two

(Practice of the formation of 'yes/no' interrogatives, and short form answers)

a Is the calendar in the; it isn't; It is on the floor.
b Are the glasses; they aren't; They are 70p. each.
c Is the Kremlin in; it isn't; It is in Moscow.
d Is the pen on the; it isn't; It is on the chair.
e Is the White House in; it isn't; It is in Washington.

Exercise three

(Practice of prepositions)

a from   c in _____ with   e of _____ on
b in _____ on   d on _____ near   f near

Exercise four

(Practice of word order)

a Where are the blue plates?
b The English books are in the bottom drawer.
c John is not very tall.
d He is a young man.
e Is the hotel near the railway station? (Is the railway station near the hotel?)
f The Arcadia is a cinema.

Exercise five

(Vocabulary)

hotel	desk	cup
church	table	saucer
petrol station	chair	plate
bus station	shelf	glass

calculator	carrot
typewriter	lettuce
telephone	tomato
clock	apple

Exercise six

a tomatoes   d The
b I   e These
c is   f She

Exercise seven

(Practice of definite and indefinite articles)

a _____ the _____ ; a _____ a _____ a; the _____ the; an _____ a

Exercise eight

these; This _____ that; This _____ that; Those _____ the

Unit four

This unit is designed to introduce and provide practice of the possessive adjectives (except 'our' and 'their'), questions with 'What . . . . . like?', the preposition 'under' and vocabulary groups associated with clothing, weather and the months of the year.

PRONUNCIATION MODELS

Her shoes are under the bed. /hə ˈʃuːz ər ʌndə ðə ˋbed/
Where's his shirt? /ˈweəz hiz ˋʃəːt/
Is Jane your daughter? /iz ˈdʒein jɔː ˌdɔːtə/
What's the weather like in January? /ˈwɔts ðə ˈweðə laik in ˋdʒænjuəri/

Exercise one

(Presentation and oral practice of a new group of vocabulary items)
The meanings of these words are best clarified by reference to real articles of clothing or picture cards in the classroom. This exercise provides useful practice of the letters 'a' to 'i', which can be used as cues in repetition practice.

Exercise two ①
(A)

(Aural comprehension practice involving 'his' and 'her', the new vocabulary, and familiarization with the pictures and the prepositions 'under' 'in' and 'on')
The suggested sentences are:

1 Her shoes are on the bed.	F
2 Her coat is in the cupboard.	T
3 His hat is in the cupboard.	F
4 His glasses are in his hand.	F
5 His trousers are on the floor.	T
6 Her hat is under the table.	F
7 His bag is on the table.	T
8 His shirt is under the bed.	F

Note 'His' and 'her' should not be stressed in this exercise.

Exercise three
(D)

(Further practice of the new vocabulary, of questions with 'where' and some prepositions, and oral practice of the distinction between the use of 'his' and the use of 'her')

17

Practice can be extended by exploiting the classroom situation. A student of each sex can be brought to the front and their respective belongings (bags, coats, pens, etc.) distributed around the classroom. It should then be possible to generate practice of the following sort:

Student 1 Where's her comb?
Student 2 On the desk.
Student 3 Are his books in his bag?
Student 4 No, they aren't.
Student 3 Where are they?
Student 4 Under her chair.
Student 5 What colour is her coat? Etc.

Exercise four
(E)

(Writing practice of new vocabulary and 'his' and 'her')
The anticipated completions are as follows:
a Her _____ his
b Her hat; his shirt
c His shoes; shoes
d Her _____ her blouse
e Where _____ his; It is _____ the table

Exercise five ⓣ
(A)

(Listening practice, and familiarization with the illustration and new vocabulary)
If necessary, students should be shown how the family tree works before being asked to do the exercise.
The suggested sentences are:
1 His mother is a housewife.   T
2 Frederick is his brother.   T
3 His son is a doctor.   F
4 Mary isn't his sister.   F
5 George is his son.   F
6 His wife is a secretary.   T
7 His daughter isn't a secretary.   T
8 Mabel is his wife.   F

Exercise six
(C)

(Oral practice of the new vocabulary groups: professions and relationships)
Some students may enjoy inventing new family trees in groups to supplement the one provided. This can be done in groups or pairs after an initial spell of intensive practice with the new vocabulary.

Exercise seven
(C)

(Further oral practice with the new vocabulary; introduction and practice of 'my')
Teachers may wish to invite students to bring photographs of members of their families. Students may then be asked to produce series of connected sentences

such as the following:

Student 1 This is my sister. Her name's Ana. She's a
secretary.

In addition, students could be invited to ask and answer
questions about the photos like this:

Student 1 Who's that (this), Ali?
Student 2 My brother.
Student 1 What's his name?
Student 2 Gaddi.
Student 1 Is he a student?
Student 2 No, he isn't. He's a mechanic. Etc.

This kind of practice serves as the beginnings of
'conversation' in English, and it is important to take
advantage of any opportunity for it that may present
itself.

Note Students will almost certainly want to know words
for relationships and professions which have not been
covered in the unit. Teachers should be ready to provide
them as they are needed.

Exercise eight ①
(F)

(Introduction and oral practice of 'your'; further practice
with the vocabulary)

Here and in the next exercise students are required to
take the roles of John (see the family tree) and one of his
friends. Practice can quickly be extended to involve
students' own relations and their professions.

Exercise nine ①
(F)

(Further oral practice of possessive adjectives and
'Who . . .?')

Students may be asked to prepare and rehearse a
dialogue based on the family tree before acting it out in
front of the class.

Exercise ten
(E)

(Writing practice of 'his' and 'her')

The anticipated completions are:

a her
b a; his _____ a
c is a; his; a music teacher

Exercise eleven
(E)

(Writing practice of possessive adjectives)

The anticipated completions are :

my; your; my; your; Her

Exercise twelve

(Introduction and oral repetition of adjectives of
temperature and the months of the year)

A calendar may be used to practise the names of the
months in English. Some teachers may wish to extend

practice of these by introducing the word 'birthday' and the question 'When . . . ?' This will give rise to the following question/answer practice

Student 1 When's your birthday, Francoise?
Student 2 (It's) in February.
or, if teachers wish to practise dates at this stage:
Student 2 (It's) on February 22nd.

Exercise thirteen ⓣ

(Aural comprehension practice involving the new adjectives; familiarization with the climate chart)
The suggested sentences are:

1	It's hot in Moscow in January.	F
2	In Buenos Aires it's wet in January.	T
3	In Montreal it's wet in July.	T
4	It's hot and very dry in Bombay in January.	T
5	It's warm in Montreal in January.	F
6	It's very wet in Buenos Aires in January.	F
7	It's very cold in Montreal in January.	T
8	It's cool and very wet in Bombay in July.	F
9	It's hot and very wet in Bombay in January.	F
10	In Buenos Aires it's dry in July.	T

Exercise fourteen (D)

(Introduction and oral practice of 'What . . . like?')
After intensive practice of examples generated by the chart, students should be asked to converse about other cities they know. Their conversation could take the following form:

Student 1 What's the weather like in . . . ., Yuki?
Student 2 Well, it's warm in August and September but it's very cold in November and December.
Student 1 Is it wet in August?
Student 2 No, it isn't. It's dry. Etc.

Exercise fifteen ⓣ **(F)**

(Introduction of 'It's a pleasure' and 'Have a good trip'; further practice of 'What . . . like?')
Students should note the relationship between the 'Here is . . . ' at the beginning of this dialogue and 'Here you are' in Unit One.

Exercise sixteen (E)

(Writing practice of 'What . . . like?' and new adjectives)
The anticipated completions are:
a What _____ like; It _____ cold
b What is the weather like; It is hot and wet
c In Bombay in July; It is

Exercise seventeen

(Extended writing practice)

This exercise will need some preparation: to make practice interesting, teachers may wish to make a list of the cities which their students are able to write about. These can be assigned to pairs of students or to individuals who can then begin preparation of their short paragraphs.

Note Students will find extended writing exercises easier if clear examples are provided first and if they are preceded by oral practice in the same framework.

Interaction sequence ⓣ **(H)**

(Practice of 'Will you . . . . . ?' used to request action, and of some responses to it)

Each change of imagined situation will require some introduction from the teacher, e.g.:

Teacher (with appropriate mime) It's very hot in the room.

Student 1 (to another student) Will you open the door, please? Etc.

(It's cold/draughty): close the window

(You don't understand): say it again

(You don't have a pen): lend me your pen. Etc.

Students should be encouraged and expected to use this language in their classes whenever they wish to make a request of this sort.

Reading comprehension ⓣ **(G)**

The answers are as follows:

1 F	4 T	7 F
2 T	5 F	8 T
3 T	6 T	

Unit five

In this unit, the present progressive and the use of it to talk about current actions are introduced. 'Can I . . . ?' used for requesting permission, the object pronouns and vocabulary groups associated with household activities and office activities are also introduced and practised.

PRONUNCIATION MODELS

The secretary is typing a letter. /ðə 'sekritri iz 'taipiŋ ə `letə/
What's the Personnel Manager doing? /wɔts ðə pə:sə`nel ˌmænədʒə du:iŋ/
Jane's helping her. /'dʒeinz `helpiŋ hə:/
Is Jim helping them? /iz 'dʒim `helpiŋ ðəm/
They aren't watching him. /ðei 'ɑ:nt `wɔtʃiŋ him/
Can I see the Accountant, please? /kæn ai si: ði: əˌkauntənt 'pli:z/

Exercise one (C)

(Introduction and oral practice of the affirmative of the present progressive)

Many teachers will wish to present some of the new verbs and the use of the present progressive to refer to current activities. This can be done by exploiting the classroom situation before beginning the exercise. Introduction of the company posts may cause some students a little difficulty. This can be overcome by means of a simple diagram of company departments: accounts, sales, personnel and production.
Note Students need not be discouraged from using a dictionary when the exact meaning of a word is causing them worry.

Exercise two (D)

(Introduction of the 'What . . . doing?' question and further practice of affirmative sentences in the present progressive)

This activity can be made more communicative if students are asked to close their books and work from memory or from enlarged pictures without captions.

Exercise three ⓣ (F)

(Introduction of 'Can I . . . .?' and further practice of the present progressive)

This exchange illustrates a common use of the present progressive. It should be acted out as realistically as possible. Students may be divided into groups of three in which one takes the part of the secretary, one that of the visitor and the other that of the person who is busy.

Exercise four
(E)

(Writing practice of the present progressive)
The anticipated completions are:
a is_____ a report
b is answering the telephone
c The _____ is talking to a customer
d The Personnel Manager is
e is the Production Manager; is visiting the
f is _____ doing; is typing a letter

Exercise five ①
(A)

(Aural comprehension practice to introduce the new vocabulary, and the information in the illustrations)
In this case quite a lot of new vocabulary is introduced. However, the meaning of it should be clear from the drawing. Teachers may wish to introduce the names of the rooms before doing exercise 5. This can be done with simple question-answer practice:

Student 1 Where's Rupert?
Student 2 In the kitchen.
Student 3 Where are Nick and Peter?
Student 4 In the big bedroom. Etc.

The suggested sentences are:

1	Donald is in the living room.	T
2	Rupert is playing the guitar.	F
3	The living room is on the ground floor.	T
4	Jill is cooking her breakfast.	F
5	Peter and Nick are doing their homework.	T
6	Mrs Black is eating her breakfast.	T
7	Ann is in the bathroom.	F
8	Mr Black is in the dining room. He is eating his breakfast.	F
9	Bill and Fred are singing their new song.	F
10	Richard is listening to Donald and Mary.	T

Exercise six
(D)

(Practice of some new vocabulary; further practice of 'on the right' and 'on the left')
'Ground floor' and 'first floor' are new to the students. Teachers may wish to extend this exercise by getting students to talk about their own homes instead of the pictures.

Exercise seven **(C)**	(Further practice of the present progressive; practice of new vocabulary and the object pronouns) Students may need a certain amount of repetition practice of the new vocabulary at the beginning of this activity. This will enable them to describe the activities in a given room more fluently. **Note** The object pronouns are generally unstressed; students should practise the weak forms.
Exercise eight **(D)**	(Introduction of 'Is . . . . . ____ ing . . . . ?'; further practice of present progressive) This exercise provides further practice of all forms of the present progressive. Students should be encouraged to mix the question types: 'What . . . . doing?', 'Where . . . ____ ing', 'Is . . . . ____ ing?', 'Are . . . . ____ ing?', 'Who is . . . . ____ ing?' etc. This would also be a good place to practise negative sentences thoroughly. The teacher and the students may make incorrect statements about the picture: *Student 1* Mr Black is eating his breakfast. *Student 2* He isn't eating his breakfast. He's talking to his wife. Etc.
Exercise nine **(E)**	(Writing practice of the present progressive and of object pronouns) The anticipated completions are: is eating her ____ in the ____ is ____ to her; are ____ the big bedroom ____ their ____ helping them; are in; singing their ____ is listening to them
Exercise ten ⓣ **(F)**	(Further practice of present progressive with questions of location) It should be imagined that speaker A is any friend of any individual in the family and that B is another member of the family who does not appear in the illustration. **Note** 'alone' is a new word.

Exercise eleven ⓣ **(F)**	(Further practice of present progressive, particularly first person, and of 'Can I . . . . ?')
	    Activities, like this one, involving the telephone are fairly common in *'Contemporary English'*. Teachers may wish to bring model phones into the classroom to make practice more realistic. Expressions like 'Is that you, Nick?' and 'Just a minute' are particularly associated with phone conversations, and students should be made to realize this.
	    Exercises 10 and 11 are both particularly suited to pair

or group work.

Exercise twelve ⑦
(F or D)

(Further oral practice)
This activity provides an opportunity to practise quite a lot of the language from Unit Three together with the present progressive in relation to a new 'situation'. Only the vocabulary will be new. Teachers may wish to extend the activity by bringing, or asking students to bring, pictures of famous people taken from magazines, etc.

Exercise thirteen
(E)

(Further writing practice)
The completions b), c) and d) should all be modelled on a):
a actress _____ France; 28 years; putting on make-up
b is a cameraman from Mexico; He is 35 years old. He is putting the film in the camera.
c is a director from Italy; He is 76 years old. He is studying the script with the star.
d is an actress from Britain; She is 22 years old. She is talking to the director.
e How old is
f Is she
g is she doing

Exercise fourteen ⑦
(A)

(Aural comprehension practice of distinction between affirmative, negative and interrogative sentence types)
The suggested sentences are:
1 Gloria is an actress.
2 Is Nick reading a book?
3 Rupert is cooking.
4 Fred isn't working at the moment.
5 You can't see the Accountant.
6 Can I speak to Richard?
7 Where is Mrs Black having her breakfast?
8 Pedro isn't Italian.
9 Who is talking to the director?
10 Donald and Mary are singing.
The sentences should be said at normal speed and students should realize that this time they do not need to look at an illustration or remember facts. They should decide which are interrogative or negative by noticing grammatical clues and differences of stress and intonation.

Interaction
sequence
(H)

(Introduction and practice of ways of asking for help with the language)
Many teachers will prefer to get students to practise Sequence A by asking for translations:

Student 1 How do you say 'bigote' in English?
Teacher (or Student 2) Moustache.
Student 3 How do you say 'Blume' in English?
Teacher (or Student 4) Flower. Etc.

In Sequence B the final response can also be in another language.

Reading comprehension ①
(G)

The answers are as follows:

1 No	4 Yes	7 Yes
2 No	5 No	8 No
3 Yes	6 No	9 No

Teachers may wish to follow the reading comprehension work with some simple conversation about other large cities that students know. Postcards and other photos would be very useful as stimuli.

Unit six

In this unit the model 'can' (can't) is introduced and
practised in connection with the idea of ability or skill.
(The use of 'can' in requests has been familiar since its
introduction in Unit One.) Time expressions and the
question 'What time is it . . . ?' are also introduced.

PRONUNCIATION MODELS

John can ride a bicycle. /ˈdʒɔn kn̩ ˈraid ə ˋbaisəkl̩/
Jane and Mary can't swim. /ˈdʒein ən ˈmeəri ˈkɑːnt ˋswim/
Can Jennifer speak French? /kn̩ ˈdʒenifə ˈspiːk ˋfrentʃ/
Yes, she can. /jes ʃi ˋkæn/
What time is it in London? /ˈwɔt ˈtaim iz it in ˋlʌndən/

Exercise one ⓣ
(A)

(Introduction and aural comprehension practice with 'can'
and 'can't'; opportunity to become familiar with the new
situation)
   The suggested sentences are:

1 John can play the guitar.	T
2 Jane and Mary can play chess.	F
3 John can swim.	F
4 Peter can't ride a bicycle.	T
5 Jane and Mary can't knit.	F
6 Carol can't speak Spanish.	F
7 John can ride a bicycle.	T
8 Peter can't play chess.	F
9 Carol can't play chess.	T
10 Carol can play the guitar.	F

Note It is important to read these sentences with
appropriate stress, i.e. 'can' is unstressed and usually
pronounced /kn/ while 'can't' is stressed.

Exercise two
(C)

(First oral practice of 'can' and 'can't' indicating ability in
affirmative and negative sentences)
   As soon as possible students can be encouraged to
produce compound sentences with 'but' contrasting 'can'
and 'can't' (see the second and third examples).

Exercise three ⓣ
(D)

(Oral practice of 'can' in questions and short answers)
   This easy exercise covering two different kinds of

27

question provides an opportunity for ensuring that students are able to use the two main kinds of question intonation (falling for the 'Who' and other 'Wh. . .' questions and falling-rising for the 'Can . . .?' question and other yes-no questions). The exercise can be extended to four 'phrases':

Student 1 How old is Carol?
Student 2 Fourteen.
Student 1 Can she ride a bicycle?
Student 2 No, she can't.

Note 'can' in the short answer 'Yes, he can' must be stressed.

Exercise four
(D)

(Further oral practice of 'can' and 'can't'; personalization)
This sort of activity is best done in pairs or groups. Teachers should expect to answer plenty of questions about vocabulary apart from that suggested in the box, and should ensure that students use the phrases practised in Interaction Sequence 3. This activity can be extended into something more like 'conversation' by introducing 'let's':

Student 1 Can you play tennis, Yukio?
Student 2 Yes I can, but not very well.
Student 1 Let's play on Friday afternoon.
Student 2 O.K. Where?
Student 1 In . . . . .

This would also provide an informal opportunity to introduce 'What time?'.

Exercise five
(B)

(Reading comprehension practice)
This exercise may be done at home and checked against a model on the board in class.

Exercise six ⓣ
(C)

(Further oral practice with 'can' and 'can't')
Students will need some repetition practice of the new vocabulary particularly the adverb 'quickly'.

Exercise seven
(D)

(Further oral practice of questions with 'can')
This can be made more interesting by asking students to close their books or cover the application forms. The 'Who . . .?' question of exercise 3 can also be practised, as can questions from previous units:

Student 1 How old is Jennifer Collins?
Student 2 21.
Student 1 Where's she from?
Student 2 North Mimms.
Student 1 Can she type quickly? Etc.

Teachers may wish to compose a similar application form suitable to their students' needs asking about different skills (e.g. swimming, driving, cooking, knitting, etc.) which can be distributed to students in pairs or groups. Students can then take it in turns to fill out each other's application forms. Beside each activity, boxes can be supplied for the categories:

e.g. swimming

Yes ☐	No ☐
very well well not very well	

Exercise eight (E)

(Oral and writing practice of 'can' and 'can't')
Before beginning the 'composition' exercise, students can be asked to say four or five consecutive and connected sentences about the four candidates. Then, after completion of exercise 8, students can be asked to produce similar paragraphs in groups about Jennifer and Rosa.
The anticipated completions are:
18 years old; is from; can ___ can speak; cannot take ___ cannot drive___ can

Exercise nine

(Repetition practice of time expressions)
It will be noted that students are not asked to say the more complex time expressions involving 'half', 'quarter', 'past' and 'to' at this stage. However, students will need to understand these expressions, and many teachers may prefer to get students to use them in this exercise and exercise 12.

Exercise ten

(Familiarization with the time chart)
Exercise 12 can be begun at this point as students work out the missing times. These are as follows:
Rio/Buenos Aires B 04.20; C 06.45
Mexico City/Chicago B 01.20; D 11.26
Moscow/Mecca C 12.45; D 20.26

Exercise eleven

(Completion of time chart)
This can be used for oral practice in the following way:
Teacher   What time is it now?
Student 1   It's nine fifteen.
Teacher   And what time is it in Mexico City?
Student 2   It's three fifteen
Teacher   Imagine it's nine o'clock in Mexico City. What time is it here? Etc.

29

Exercise twelve Ⓣ
(D)

(Oral practice of time expressions)
   The more complex time expressions listed in the box for reference should be mixed freely with simple time expressions if students are being expected to master both sets. In that case students may need a little more time to formulate their answers than in previous activities.

Exercise thirteen
(E)

(Writing practice of time expressions)
   In this exercise students are expected to use both kinds of time expression as the exercise indicates.
   The anticipated completions are:
a   What time is; (It is) (a) _____ to four
b   What time is it; is three o'clock (or three p.m.)
c   time is it in Rio (Buenos Aires; It is
d   What time is it in Chicago (Mexico City); _____ It is
e   It is one twenty (a.m.)

Interaction
sequence Ⓣ
(F)

(Oral practice of expressions used in greeting and leave-taking)
   Many of these expressions will be 'known' to the students. It is important to ensure that they understand exactly when they are used and how they are pronounced. These expressions can then be used naturally at the beginning and end of future classes.

Reading
comprehension Ⓣ
(G)

The facts in this reading comprehension are true, and students may be invited to find out more about the Bushmen and similar groups using their own reference books or those in a library.
   The answers are:

| 1 F | 3 F | 5 F | 7 F |
| 2 T | 4 T | 6 T | 8 F |

Second review and complementation unit

In this unit the personal pronouns are listed and practised in two revision exercises. Teachers will need to begin by some classroom oral practice of those pronouns which have not occurred in the previous units, which are the first person object pronouns, and the possessive pronouns.

Below are some suggestions for the introduction and practice of these in simple classroom activities:

Me/Us/You A simple mime game involving two or three people can provide practice of these words and revision of the present progressive. A student or a pair of students mime(s) an activity, preferably one associated with vocabulary students already know. Another student asks questions:

Student 1 Are you writing a letter, Francoise?
Student 2 No, I'm not.
Student 1 What are you doing?
Student 2 I'm doing my homework.
Student 1 And what's Mario doing?
Student 2 He's helping me.

By increasing the number of people miming actions, 'us' can be practised:

Student 3 What are you and Hans doing, Ulrike?
Student 4 We're cooking the breakfast.
Student 3 And what's Julia doing?
Student 4 She's watching us.

Then the dialogue can be reversed.

Student 5 What am I doing, Jose?
Student 6 You're singing a song.
Student 5 And what's Hisako doing?
Student 6 She's listening to you. Etc.

By alternately using these 'multiphase' drills and others like them, teachers should be able to provide sufficient practice of these and other object pronouns.

Mine/Yours/His/Hers, etc. Practice of this set of pronouns can be done by using students' possessions. A mixture of possessions, including several lighters, pens, bags, etc. can be collected and placed at the front of the classroom. Then students can take it in turns to ask and

answer questions (this exercise can also provide revision practice of 'this', 'that', 'these' and 'those').
Student 1 Is this comb yours, Carlos?
Student 2 No, it isn't. Ask Claude. I think it's his. Etc.
  More than one object can be indicated to facilitate practice of 'ours' and 'theirs':
Student 3 Are these books ours, Sara?
Student 4 No, they aren't. Ask Maria and Jorge. I think they are theirs. Etc.
Note The introduction of the phrases 'Ask . . .' and 'I think . . .' should cause no trouble and may prove useful in the remaining units of the book. They are necessary here to avoid the unnatural use of 'his', 'hers' and 'theirs' to refer to persons whose names are known to the speaker. If students in the class do not know each other's names, pronouns alone may be used with a pointing gesture, but students should understand that this is not normal practice in English in the hearing of the person indicated.

  The following is a brief key to the exercises in this unit:

Exercise one

(Practice of pronouns; subject, object and possessive pronouns and possessive adjectives)
you; you; I_____ my; They; their, your; He; Their; my; She; Her, your; yours; His; his_____ hers

Exercise two

a its	d their_____them	g him
b me	e us	h ours; yours
c her	f Our	

Exercise three

(Further practice of times)
o, a, m, i, d, n, g, f, h, c, k, l, b, j, e

Exercise four

(Vocabulary)

living room	doctor	shirt
dining room	secretary	trousers
kitchen	carpenter	hat
bedroom	writer	blouse
bathroom	accountant	coat

hot	speak
cool	write
warm	talk
wet	answer
cold	read

Exercise five

(Practice of 'can' and the present progressive)
Can I; is playing; Are_____playing; can't_____can read;
She can; are_____doing; am cooking; Can you;
Are_____studying; am not; am studying; can't; Can

Exercise six

(Cumulative oral practice)
   In this activity a student should be selected and asked
to choose an identity from the table. He should not tell
anybody which name he has selected, and perhaps it is
better for him to sit or stand at the front of the
classroom. All the other students should then try to work
out by interrogation who he is. They will need to ask
questions about his age, work and hometown, and about
the weather in his hometown in order to be certain of his
identity. The person who guesses his identity then chooses
a name for herself/himself and comes to the front.
Note The question 'Who are you?' should be avoided
except in desperation.

Unit seven

This is the first in a series of four units concerned with the present simple. Here the third person singular form is introduced and practised in affirmative, negative and interrogative sentences with reference to routine actions and occurrences. The question word 'How' is also introduced as well as prepositional phrases with 'by' to describe transportation.

PRONUNCIATION MODELS

Flight 309 goes to Paris. /flait ˈθriː ˈou ˈnain ˈgouz tə ˋpæris/
It stops in Miami. /it ˈstɔps in maiˋjæmi/
How does Stephen travel to Battersea? /ˈhau dəz ˈstiːvn̩ ˈtrævl̩ tə ˋbætəsiː/
What time does Ann begin work? /ˈwɔt ˈtaim dəz ˈæn biˈgin ˋwəːk/
Does Jack live in Croydon? /dəz ˈdʒæk ˈliv in ˌkroidn̩/

Exercise one ⓉT
(A)
(Aural comprehension practice of present simple; familiarization with the timetable)

While requiring that students look at the timetable closely, this exercise provides students with an opportunity to become familiar with several related verbs (get to, stop at, reach, arrive, etc). It is for individual teachers to decide whether they should activate all these verbs that appear in the examples.

The suggested sentences are:

1	Flight 309 goes to Paris.	D
2	Flight 873 stops in Detroit.	V
3	Flight 714 arrives in New York at 11.45.	D
4	Flight 312 stops in Bermuda.	V
5	Flight 603 goes to St. Louis.	V
6	Flight 873 leaves at five past seven.	Dp
7	Flight 603 departs at 2.30.	Dp
8	Flight 312 arrives in London at 7.55.	A
9	Flight 873 gets to Montreal at ten to ten.	A
10	Flight 603 reaches Chicago at a quarter to five.	A

Exercise two **(C)**	(Oral practice of the present simple, third person singular in affirmative sentences) This activity provides an opportunity for students to become accustomed to using this new form of the verb and to revise time expressions. As soon as possible students should be invited to string sentences together: e.g. 'Flight seven one four goes to New York. It leaves at a quarter past eight. It stops in Dallas, and arrives in New York at a quarter to twelve.' **Note** In this and the following two exercises students need to become familiar with two types of verb ending: 'leaves' 'goes' and 'arrives' are all pronounced with a final /z/ whereas 'stops' is pronounced with a final /s/.
Exercise three ① **(D)**	(Oral practice of present simple–questions and answers) In this exercise students are asked to produce the present tense auxiliary 'does' for the first time. Students are likely to have some difficulty. a with the new infinitive form of the verb following 'does', particularly since they have just practised a form of the verb ending in 's', and b with the varying pronunciation of 'does' depending on whether it is unstressed (/dəz/) or stressed as it is in the short answer 'Yes, he does' (/dʌz/). In this activity, as in others of the same kind, an element of realistic communicativeness can be added by asking half of the class, who will be asking questions, to close their books. This can be extended to a problem-solving activity with a new timetable: students are given a variety of cards. Each card contains a flight number (or bus number) and one piece of information about it under one of the four headings in the timetable in the book. Individual students move round the class asking questions to complete the information missing on his card. If he asks the wrong person (someone who does not have the information) he will receive the answer 'I don't know' and perhaps 'Ask . . .'. If he receives an appropriate answer he should fill in the information on his card, and continue his search.
Exercise four **(E)**	(Writing practice of present simple – third person singular) The anticipated completions are: a 309; Miami b 603 leaves_____ arrives_____ at c does flight 312 leave d stop in e stop in Dallas, Detroit etc.

Exercise five ⓣ
(B)

(Aural comprehension practice; familiarization with the map)

Before beginning this activity it is advisable to go over the short paragraph about Stephen showing students how the map and the symbols and times on it work. After students have understood this and looked at the map for a short time it should be possible for them to fill in names, professions and times without difficulty as they become gradually familiar with the new vocabulary. However a little time should be given between the reading of each sentence to allow students to write in the necessary data.

The words 'engineer', 'factory' and 'secretary' should be written on the board, not necessarily in this order, before reading the sentences.

The recommended sentences are as follows:

1 Jack is an engineer.
2 Janice arrives home at one o'clock.
3 Jack works in a factory in Lambeth.
4 Ann is a secretary.
5 She finishes work at 5.15.

Exercise six ⓣ
(A)

(Revision of 'north' and 'south' and further aural comprehension)

It should be made very clear that students need to decide whether the action mentioned in each sentence takes place north of the River Thames or south of it.

The recommended sentences are:

1 Stephen arrives home at 5.30.   N
2 Janice studies in Notting Hill.   N
3 Jack works in Lambeth.   S
4 Ann leaves home at 8.15 in the morning.   S
5 Ann works in Islington.   N

Exercise seven
(C)

(Oral practice of the present simple, affirmative and negative)

Although examples are not given in the exercise, many teachers will find this a good opportunity to begin practice of the present simple in negative sentences. This can be done naturally in the following way:

Student 1 Janice leaves home at 8 o'clock.
Student 2 Ann doesn't leave home at 8 o'clock: she leaves at 8.15. Etc.

As soon as it is convenient, students should be encouraged to say all they can about a given character, imitating the short paragraph about Stephen.

Note A third type of verb ending is introduced here: 'finishes' and 'teaches' are pronounced with a final extra syllable /iz/.

<table>
<tr><td>Exercise eight ⓣ
(D)</td><td>(Further oral practice of questions and answers in the present simple; introduction of the question word 'How')
    Many teachers may wish to reverse the order of exercises 7 and 8 in order to make practice of these various questions more natural. There seem to be few disadvantages in this, provided students are asked at some stage to produce full affirmative sentences of the kind suggested in exercise 7.
    This activity can very easily be 'personalized' by getting students to ask similar questions (and perhaps take note of the answers) about other students' brothers, sisters, etc. This can best be done in pairs or small groups.</td></tr>
</table>

Exercise nine
(E)

(Writing practice of the present simple and new vocabulary)
    The anticipated completions are:
a does _____ arrive at
b Where does _____ live
c How does _____ travel
d What time does _____ arrive
e Does Jack work
f How does Stephen travel to work
g Where does Ann work
h Does Stephen live in

Exercise ten

(Composition writing)
    Students are here asked to write down a logical sequence of connected sentences about a relative. This will clearly be easier if students are invited to prepare this orally. Many students will ask for help with vocabulary and should try to use the expressions learnt in Unit Three.

Exercise eleven ⓣ
(F)

(Cumulative oral practice; revision of 'can' and several other items)
    After repetition drilling students should be allowed to prepare alternative versions in pairs or groups. This can be extended to cover museums, etc. in the students' environment.

Exercise twelve
(E)

(Guided composition practice)
    This sort of exercise can be left for homework, since there is little that can go wrong provided students understand clearly the task. Again students might be requested to prepare a third paragraph about a museum, etc. in their environment.

Interaction
sequence ⊤
(F)

(Introduction and oral practice of one way of making invitations)

This interaction sequence also introduces several other new items: a group of vocabulary items to do with entertainment, the days of the week, the use of the present simple with 'I', the adverbials 'today', 'tomorrow' and 'tonight', a way of refusing invitations and a way of accepting them, etc. This will mean that students may need a little more help than usual

a with comprehension and pronunciation
b with working out variations.

Reading
comprehension ⊤
(G)

The names associated with the British Isles cause some confusion both in English and in other languages. The United Kingdom is best understood as a federation of countries, each with its own history and culture. Great Britain includes only three of these countries: England, Scotland and Wales. Southern Ireland, usually known as the Republic of Ireland or Eire is an entirely independent nation, the capital of which is Dublin. (London is the capital of the United Kingdom, Great Britain and England, Whilst Edinburgh is the capital of Scotland, Cardiff the capital of Wales, and Belfast the capital of Northern Ireland). More information about these political, geographical and cultural divisions can be found in the 'Handbook to Britain', published by H.M.S.O. and available in most British and British Council libraries.

The answers to the questions are:

1 g	3 a	5 c	7 h
2 d	4 b	6 e	8 f

Unit eight

In this unit the present simple tense (affirmative, negative and interrogative) is practised with other kinds of subject (not third person singular), and the forms 'do' and 'don't' are introduced. Here the present tense is used to describe characteristics as well as to talk about routines. The question 'How much . . . . ?' is introduced.

PRONUNCIATION MODELS

Pumas eat meat. /ˈpjuːməz ˈiːt ˈmɪːt/
What do cheetahs eat? /ˈwɔt duː ˈtʃiːtəz ˌiːt/
The Garcias don't live in a house. /ðə ˈgɑːsiəz ˈdount ˈliv in ə ˈhaus/
How much do the Satos earn? /ˈhau ˈmʌtʃ duː ðə ˈsætouz ˌəːn/

Exercise one ①
(A)

(Aural comprehension practice with present simple and new vocabulary; familiarization with the information to be used in oral practice)
The information to be used in practice contains a considerable amount of new vocabulary. However, with a minimum of assistance, explanation and translation students will be able to understand it.
The suggested sentences are:

1	Pumas live in mountains and forests.	T
2	Chimpanzees eat meat.	F
3	Cheetahs eat meat.	T
4	Cheetahs weight about 45 kilos.	T
5	Pumas don't eat meat.	F
6	Chimpanzees weigh about 25 kilos.	F
7	Chimpanzees and baboons eat fruit.	T
8	Pumas weigh about 70 kilos.	T
9	Cheetahs don't live in Africa.	F
10	Chimpanzees and baboons live in Africa.	T

Exercise two
(C)

(Oral practice of the present simple with plural subject)
After repetition practice of new vocabulary, students should be asked to give information about the animals both in affirmative and in negative sentences. Teachers may wish to extend practice to include other animals.

39

After looking up the relevant information in an encyclopaedia, charts similar to those in the book can be put on the board. Alternatively students can be asked to look up information about animals of their choice and report to the class in a later lesson.

**Exercise three
(D)**

(Oral practice of questions and answers in the present simple — third person plural; introduction of 'How much......?')

Here practice can be made more communicative by asking some students to close their books. In addition, students may ask each other questions about the animals they have looked up at home.

Note Except in short answers (Yes, they do) 'do' is generally unstressed and pronounced /də`/.

**Exercise four
(E)**

(Writing practice of the present simple—third person plural)

The anticipated completions are:

a live; do not live   d do____eat
b weigh; eat   e do____live
c live; weigh

**Exercise five ⓣ
(B)**

(Aural comprehension practice of the present simple, familiarization with the information to be used in oral practice)

Students may need to be shown how the table of information works before the exercise is begun.

1 The Satos get up at 6.30.
2 The Garcias earn 600 dollars a month.
3 The Satos spend 375 dollars a month on rent.
4 The Sinclairs earn 1,800 dollars a month.
5 Their children go to work at 9 a.m.

**Exercise six ⓣ
(A)**

(Aural comprehension practice of the present simple)

The suggested sentences are:

1 The Garcias get up at 8 a.m.   T
2 The Satos live in a mobile home.   F
3 The Garcias have four children.   T
4 The Sinclairs spend 1,800 dollars a month
   on rent.   F
5 The Satos earn 1,000 dollars a month.   T

Exercise seven ⓣ

(Reading comprehension)

This exercise may be done at home and checked against a model on the board in class.

Exercise eight
(C)

(Further oral practice of the present simple, third person plural)

After the usual practice of affirmative and negative sentences, students may be asked to say three or four connected sentences about one of the families.

Note Some teachers may prefer to reverse exercises 8 and 9.

Exercise nine Ⓣ
(D)

(Further oral practice of the present simple, third person plural, questions and answers)

It is important to ensure that students practise all the various questions suggested.

Note 'How much' is here used with reference to money, whereas in exercise 3 it was used with reference to weight.

Exercise ten
(E)

(Writing practice of the present simple)

The anticipated completions are:

live _____ near; get up; do not eat; go _____ at; earn _____ spend 375 dollars a month

Exercise eleven

(Further writing practice of the present simple)

Students may be asked to do this exercise in pairs or groups. They should be encouraged to follow the model paragraph closely.

Exercise twelve

(Reading comprehension practice)

This exercise provides an opportunity for students to practise reading the recently introduced present simple together with items from previous units, and to become familiar with the dialogue to be practised in exercise 13.

Exercise thirteen
(F)

a) (Further cumulative oral practice)

Students may begin by practising the dialogue in exercise 12 in pairs and then work out new dialogues on the basis of forms B and C. Many teachers will wish to exploit this activity to provide more practice of the present simple, third person singular. This can be done in the following way:

Student 1 Where does Jim Williams live?
Student 2 At number 13, Malden Drive.
Student 1 How old is he?
Student 2 45.
Student 1 What does he do? Etc.

b) (Oral comprehension practice)

Students may need to listen to the dialogue on tape two or three times before filling out the form, which they should copy carefully.

Exercise fourteen (F)

(Further cumulative oral practice)
This activity can also be followed up with practice of the third person singular, present tense. Students can be asked by others about the person they interviewed. In addition, further forms can be filled out recording information about students' relatives, etc.

Interaction sequence ⓣ (H)

(Introduction and practice of some ways of complaining and apologizing)
This interaction sequence can easily be acted out in class with personal possessions.
Note In many situations it is possible to shorten 'That's my suitcase you're taking' to simply 'That's my suitcase'.

Reading comprehension ⓣ (G)

A The answers are:

| 1 F | 2 T | 3 T | 4 F |
| 5 T | 6 T | 7 F | 8 F |

B The anticipated completions are:
1 50,000
2 Houses made of wood and turf
3 not usually tall ___ powerful legs and shoulders (a yellowish skin and straight, black hair)
4 seals
5 sled or *kayak*

The reading comprehension can be followed by further oral practice:
Student 1: Where do Eskimos live?
Student 2: In the Arctic.
Student 3: What do they eat; Etc.

Unit nine

In this unit the verb 'have' is introduced and practised, but only with the meaning of 'possess', 'contain', etc. 'Have' is practised with the auxiliary 'do' (does) in the negative and interrogative, thus allowing for plentiful practice of the distinction between 'do' (don't) and 'does' (doesn't). However, an appendix is provided at the end of the book for those teachers who prefer to teach 'have (has) got' and its interrogative and negative counterparts.

Unit Nine also provides further practice of the present simple form of other verbs. In this case the tense is used to denote habit, and the questions 'How many . . . . ?' and 'How often . . . . ?' are introduced along with some adverbials of frequency (once a week, etc.).

PRONUNCIATION MODELS

The large house has four bedrooms. /ðə ˈlɑːdʒ ˈhaus hæz ˈfɔː ˈbedrumz/

The cottages don't have garages. /ðə ˈkɔtidʒiz ˈdount hæv ˈgærɑːʒiz/

How many cups of tea does Rodney drink? /ˈhau ˈmeni ˈkʌps əv ˈtiː dəz ˈrɔdni ˈdriŋk/

How often does Harvey go to the cinema? /ˈhau ˈɔfn̩ dəz ˈhɑːvi ˈgou tə ðə ˈsinəmɑː/

Exercise one ⊤
(A)

(Aural comprehension practice of 'has' and 'have'; familiarization with the information to be used in oral practice)

The suggested sentences are:

1 The large house is in Hampstead.	F
2 The small house has two bedrooms.	F
3 The flats have small kitchens.	T
4 The cottages have two bedrooms.	F
5 The large house has two bathrooms.	T
6 The flats are in Wimbledon.	T
7 The cottages have small kitchens.	F
8 The small house has a garage.	F
9 The large house doesn't have a swimming pool.	F
10 The flats don't have gardens.	T

Exercise two **(C)**	(Oral practice of 'have' and 'has'; further oral practice of the contrast between 'don't' and 'doesn't') Students should be requested to mix affirmative and negative, and singular and plural freely.
Exercise three **(D)**	(Oral practice of 'yes/no' questions with 'do' and 'does') This activity may be extended as follows: *Student 1* Does your house have two bedrooms? *Student 2* No, it doesn't. It has three. *Student 3* Do you live in a flat? *Student 4* Yes, I do. *Student 3* Do the flats in your building have garages? *Student 4* Yes, they do. They're on the ground floor. Etc.
Exercise four **(E)**	(Writing practice of 'has' and 'have') The anticipated completions are.

a has
b do not have
c many bedrooms do

d does not have
e Does ＿＿＿ have; does
f Do ＿＿＿ have; do not

Exercise five ⓣ **(A)**	(Aural comprehension practice and familiarization with the information to be used in practice) For the first time students are asked to deal with graphs. For many this means of presenting information may be rather new; however, there is nothing difficult about them and numbers are provided inside the graph to clarify them. The suggested sentences are:

1 The average person uses 260 gallons of petrol
   a year.   M
2 The average person eats 36 kilos of meat a year.   M
3 The average person goes to the cinema 19 times
   a year.   C
4 The average person earns 1,425 dollars a month.   C
5 The average person drinks 290 cups of coffee
   a year.   M

6 Rodney drinks 75 cups of coffee a year.   T
7 Rodney uses 360 gallons of petrol a year.   F
8 Harvey goes to the cinema about once a week.   T
9 Rodney eats a lot of meat.   F
10 Harvey doesn't drink tea.   T

Exercise six **(C)**	(Further oral practice of the present simple; first practice of expressions of frequency and quantity) Two fictional countries have been used to avoid

44

inaccuracies. However, if statistics are available from government agencies, etc., many students will find it interesting to continue practice on similar lines based on factual information about their own or other countries.

Exercise seven
(C)

(Further oral practice of the present simple)
  Opportunities should be taken for continuing practice of negative sentences, by contradiction or contrast between the two individuals.

Exercise eight ⓣ
(D)

(Further oral practice of questions and answers in the present simple; introduction of 'How many . . . ?' and 'How often . . . ?')
  Practice can be done in pairs or groups in which students alternately close and open their books.

Exercise nine
(E)

(Writing practice of the present simple)
  The anticipated completions are:
  a does not eat   e How often does _____ go to; a
  b drinks _____ glasses of   f does not drink
  c does Rodney live   g goes to _____ once a year
  d much petrol does _____ use h does not work in; works in

Exercise ten
(D)

(Further oral practice – conversation)
  This activity provides an opportunity for students to practise the present simple and other language in personal conversation. Teachers may find it helpful to get students to prepare the following information on pieces of paper so that less time is spent on reflection during practice:
  I go to the cinema . . . . times a month (year).
  I play . . . . times a week (month).
  I go to . . . . times a month (year).
  I eat at a restaurant . . . . . times a year (month).
  I visit . . . . times a year (month). Etc.

Exercise eleven
(D)

(Further oral practice – conversation)
  This activity offers practice of a wide range of language, notably the contrast between third person singular and third person plural in the present simple. The conversation should be held between members of a small group. Once brothers and sisters have been talked about, conversation can continue about other members of the family, friends, etc. However, it is generally not advisable to allow this sort of activity to continue for more than ten minutes.

Exercise twelve

(Further writing practice of the present simple)
  The paragraph will need careful preparation and the

exercise is perhaps best done in pairs so that students can ask and answer the necessary questions and help each other.

Interaction sequence ⓣ (H)

(Introduction and oral practice of expressions used in offering and accepting things)
This sequence also intentionally provides practice of 'hungry' and 'thirsty' and noun phrases with 'of'. Teachers may wish to use magazine pictures stuck on cards as cues to increase the range of food and drink to be offered.

Reading comprehension ⓣ (G)

The answers are:

1 T	3 F	5 F	7 F
2 T	4 T	6 F	

(See page 52, Appendix on has/have got)

Unit ten

This unit continues practice of the present simple,
focussing particularly on those verbs (statives) which are
not used in the present (or past) progressive. These verbs
include 'cost', 'want', 'like', 'prefer' and 'mean'. In
addition adverbs of frequency (usually, often, sometimes,
etc.) are introduced and practised with the present simple,
and several prepositions used with time expressions are
also practised.

PRONUNCIATION MODELS

How much does the blender on the table cost? /ˈhau ˈmʌtʃ dəz
ðə ˈblendər ɔn ðə teibl̩ ˌkɔst/

I prefer that one. /ai priˈfə: ˈðæt wʌn/

Mr Brown never watches television in the morning. /ˈmistə
ˈbraun ˈnevə ˈwɔtʃiz ˈteliviʒn in ðə ˈmɔ:niŋ/

Mr Brown sometimes plays tennis on Sundays. /ˈmistə ˈbraun
ˈsʌmtaimz ˈpleiz ˈtenis ɔn ˈsʌndeiz/

Exercise one ⓣ
(A)

(Aural comprehension practice)

This and the following four exercises provide practice of
post-modifying prepositional phrases, e.g. the refrigerator
in the corner . . . . . This is a popular means of definition
in English, and students should understand clearly the
difference between this kind of prepositional phrase and
those which occur after the verb 'be'. (See Units One and
Five).

The suggested sentences are:

1 The refrigerator in the corner is small.   F
2 The small washing machine is near the table.   T
3 The large blender is on the shelf.   F
4 The washing machine under the shelf is big.   T

5 The refrigerator under the window costs
   95 pounds.   S
6 The toaster on the shelf costs 18 pounds.   L
7 The blender on the shelf costs 16 pounds.   S
8 The refrigerator in the corner costs 220 pounds. L

47

Exercise two **(C)**	(Oral practice of postmodifying prepositional phrases and 'cost') This exercise, which some teachers may wish to reverse with exercise 3, also provides useful revision of some numerals. Students may of course begin by saying sentences like: 'The large refrigerator costs 220 pounds'.
Exercise three **(D)**	(Further oral practice of 'How much . . . ?' and the present simple) Students may be asked to cover the price list in order to make the exercise more communicative. Later, the exercise can be extended: *Student 1* How much does a calculator cost? *Student 2* A small calculator costs about . . . . . Etc.
Exercise four ⓣ **(F)**	(Oral practice of various stative verbs, and demonstratives) The new verbs 'like', 'want', 'mean' and 'prefer' may need some illustration or explanation. As students become familiar with the dialogue, the situation can be changed to different kinds of shops (e.g. clothes, plates, etc., knives, etc.). By getting students to ask for things in the plural, it will be possible to achieve further practice of 'these' and 'those' as well as of 'this' and 'that'.
Exercise five **(E)**	(Writing practice) The anticipated completions are: a small blender d large washing machine/toaster b small ____ costs e large washing machine costs c How much ____ cost
Exercise six ⓣ **(A)**	(Aural comprehension practice of the present simple and frequency words; practice in discriminating between singular and plural; familiarization with the information to be used in oral practice) The suggested sentences are:

1 The manager sometimes changes foreign currency.   F
2 The cleaners clean the bathrooms.   T
3 The cashiers sometimes visit Head Office.   F
4 The secretary earns 4,000 pounds a year.   T
5 The cleaners begin work at 11 a.m.   F

6 Managers make loans.   P
7 A cashier receives money.   S
8 A cleaner sweeps the floor.   S
9 Secretaries type letters.   P
10 Cashiers cash cheques.   P

Note 6 to 10 do not relate closely to the information provided in the table. Students should cover the table for these items.

Exercise seven **(C)**	(Further oral practice of the present simple — third persons singular and plural; introduction of 'sometimes' and 'never') This exercise allows for practice of new vocabulary and further work on the affirmative and negative of the present simple. The exercise may be extended by encouraging students to talk about places of work or companies they are familiar with.
Exercise eight Ⓣ **(D)**	(Further oral practice of various questions in the simple present) Instead of the answers suggested in the examples, students may answer simply 'Yes, always', 'Yes, sometimes' or 'No, never'.
Exercise nine **(E)**	(Writing practice of new vocabulary and some frequency words) The anticipated completions are: a sometimes visits b never wash the c How much does; 10,000 a year (or p.a.) d What time do ___ begin e sometimes attends to
Exercise ten	(Further writing practice) It may be preferable to begin this exercise by working out a sample paragraph with the students on the board: The cashiers at the Hampton National Bank earn about 6,000 pounds a year. They begin work at 9 a.m. and finish at 4 p.m. They cash cheques and receive deposits. The cashiers sometimes change foreign currency, too. After this, students may be asked to write a similar paragraph individually or in pairs.
Exercise eleven Ⓣ **(A)**	(Aural comprehension practice of frequency words; familiarization with the information to be used in oral practice) The suggested sentences are:

1	James never reads the newspaper.	T
2	Mrs Brown always reads the newspapers at breakfast.	F
3	Sally and James often watch television on Sundays.	F
4	Mr Brown sometimes plays tennis on Sundays.	T
5	Grandmother never watches television in the morning.	F

6 They always play tennis on Saturdays.   P
7 She sometimes reads the newspaper after lunch.   S
8 He always reads the newspaper at breakfast.   S
9 They don't often watch television on Sundays.   P
10 She never plays tennis.   S
Note Students should cover the chart for 6 to 10 and
distinguish singular from plural by listening alone.

Exercise twelve
(C)

(Oral practice of the present simple and frequency words)
    Some teachers may wish to introduce one or two other
frequency words e.g. usually, generally, frequently, as
alternatives to 'often' and 'seldom' as an alternative to
'not often'.

Exercise thirteen
(D)

(Further oral practice of the present simple interrogative,
    As in exercise 8, alternative answers with frequency
words but without 'do' or 'does' or a subject are equally
acceptable. This activity should be extended to include
personalized practice:
Student 1 Do you play tennis?
Student 2 Yes, sometimes.
Student 1 When do you play?
Student 2 I sometimes play on Saturdays.
Student 1 Where? Etc.

Exercise fourteen
(E)

(Writing practice of frequency words)
    The anticipated completions are:
a always
b sometimes plays tennis
c always play tennis
d reads the newspaper
e often plays tennis

Interaction
sequence ⓣ
(H)

(Introduction and practice of one way of making an
invitation and a way of accepting an invitation)
    In role-playing students may wish to invent invitations
different from those in the book. They should be
encouraged to ask for the vocabulary they need by using
the expressions learnt in Unit Five.

Reading
comprehension ⓣ
(G)

The answers are:
A 1 T   5 T   9 F
   2 F   6 F   10 T
   3 T   7 T
   4 T   8 F

B The anticipated completions are:

1 ... about 14 million
2 ... 3 million square miles
3 ... iron ore, coal, zinc, copper, gold, silver and uranium
4 ... temperate
5 ... aborigines

Third review and complementation unit

Exercise one

In this unit no new structural items are introduced. The following is a brief key to the exercises in the unit.

(Practice of adverbs of frequency)
a   never rides _____ always ride
b   never goes _____ always visits
c   often visit _____ sometimes go
d   often rides _____ never plays
e   sometimes visits _____ never visit
f   always goes _____ often go
g   often plays _____ never rides
h   always play
i   always goes _____ never goes
j   always visits _____ never visit nightclubs at the weekend

Exercise two

(Practice of the present simple, affirmative, interrogative and negative)
a   cooks the lunch
b   walk to school
c   Does _____ play badminton; she does
d   do _____ finish school
e   does _____ do; buys
f   get up (etc.); walk to
g   Does Jack Watson eat
h   do Bob and Jeff go
i   does Mary Lewis do; reads
j   eats breakfast
k   doesn't phone; writes
l   goes home
m   does Caroline Baker begin
n   Do Bob and Jeff; finish
o   does Jack Watson do at 8 o'clock

Exercise three

(Practice of question forms with 'How', 'What', etc.)
1   How much
2   How many
3   How often
4   (At) what time
5   How old
6   How often
7   How much
8   (At) what time
9   How old
10   How many

52

Exercise four   (Practice of stative verbs)
want; do _____ like; prefer; do _____ mean; does _____ cost; costs

Exercise five   (Vocabulary)

a	pipe	f	toaster
b	cottage	g	cupboard
c	biscuit	h	cash
d	cashier	i	floor
e	postcard	j	hungry

Cumulative review exercises

The following is a brief key to the exercises.

Exercise one

(Practice of prepositions)
from _____ in _____ in; between; from; from _____ to
_____ by; at _____ in; to _____ in_____ at; at/in; In _____ of
_____ at; at, On _____ to; at _____ for; On _____ with
_____ at; to _____ for

Exercise two

(Practice of possessive adjectives)
your; my; her; my; his_____ our; your; your; his; your;
my

Exercise three

(Practice of question forms with 'How', 'What', etc.)

a	How often	e	What colour	i	Where
b	Who	f	What	j	How old
c	How	g	What time	k	How many
d	How much	h	What _____ like	l	How

Exercise four

(Vocabulary)

Town	Street	Kitchen	Office
railway station	bicycle	knives	accountant
church	bus	refrigerator	calculator
hospital	car	saucers	secretary
university	truck	stove	typewriter

Exercise five

(Practice of word order)
a John is looking at me.
b Where does your brother live?
c Can his son drive a car?
d The manager is driving a big white car.
e What time does this shop open?
f Do the students eat at the college?
g Is this book good?
h How many dogs does John have?
i Mary usually travels to work by bus.
j What is the weather like in Rio in January?
k Hans speaks English very well.
l Is the airport near the motel?

Exercise six	(Practice of present tense of 'have', 'can', and 'be')
	is ____ is; is ____ can; has ____ does not have; is ____ has,
	can; has; is; is ____ can;.are ____ have

Exercise seven   (Practice of present simple versus present progressive)

a Do you want   e do you go
b He is writing   f he is playing
c am going to clean g do you do
d do not understand h costs

Appendix on 'has/have got'

Exercise one ⓣ

(Introduction and aural comprehension practice of 'has/have got')
The suggested sentences are:

1	He's got fair hair.	B
2	She's got three children.	J
3	He's got a long moustache.	M
4	She's got brown hair.	S
5	She's got two children.	S
6	He's got a beard.	B
7	He's got one daughter.	M
8	She's got fair hair.	J

Exercise two
(C)

(Oral practice of 'has got' and 'have got')
This exercise should be exploited to provide practice of 'hasn't got' and 'haven't got' also. This can be done by providing untrue statements to be contradicted:
Student 1 Jill's got blue eyes.
Student 2 She's hasn't got blue eyes; she's got green eyes. Etc.

Exercise three
(D)

(Introduction and practice of 'What does . . . . look like?'; oral practice of 'yes/no' questions with 'has/have got')
The language practised here is commonly used in asking for and providing partial descriptions of people. The activity can be extended into conversation about students' brothers, sisters, boyfriends, wives, parents, etc., or, if students prefer, into conversation about well known actors, singers, etc.

Exercise four
(D)

(Oral practice of 'How many . . . . . ?' and 'has/have' got')
The question 'How many children have the . . . . . got?' should be alternated with 'How many children has . . . . . got?' to provide contrastive practice.

Exercise five ⓣ
(D)

a) (Further oral practice of 'have got' with other useful expressions)
In this activity and the next, students are shown additional uses of 'has/have got' (or has/have), notably temporary possession, illness or future commitment.

This dialogue also contains some preliminary exposure to 'some' and 'any' (to be dealt with in Book 2, Unit Two)

b) (Further oral practice of 'has got' and the present progressive)
In this dialogue 'why' is introduced for the first time.

General note Whether teachers prefer their students to learn 'has/have got' or 'have' with 'do/does', it is probably advisable for students to be able to comprehend both forms, since both are current in many parts of the English speaking world. 'Have' meaning 'consume' is not dealt with specifically since it operates in the same way as any other verb in the present simple. Students should understand very clearly that 'has/have got' cannot be used when 'have' means 'consume'.

Lexis list for Pupil's Book 1

R = Review Unit
P = passive language
1, 2 etc. = Unit no.

A
a (1)
a lot (9)
ability (6)
Aborigine (10P)
about (8)
accent (7P)
according to (9P)
account (n.10)
accountant (5)
accurate (8P)
across (6P)
active (3)
actor (3)
actress (3)
address (n.8)
advertisement (9P)
affair (8P)
African (6)
afternoon (7)
again (4)
age (n.8)
agricultural (7P)
airport (R3)
all (1)
all right (7)
almost (8P)
alone (5)
also (7P)
although (8P)
always (10)
am (R1)
an (1)
anaesthetic (4P)
anaesthetist (4P)

and (2)
Anglo-Saxon (7P)
animal (6P)
another (5P)
answer (v.5)
antelope (8)
any (10P)
apple (1)
application form (6)
approximately (5P)
April (4)
are (1)
area (3P)
around (9P)
arrival (7P)
arrive (7)
arrow (6P)
art gallery (3P)
artery (4P)
artesian well (10P)
as (4P)
assist (5)
assistant (2)
at (2P)
attend (10)
August (4)
autograph (3)
avenue (3P)
average (9)
away (8P)

B
baboon (8)
bacon (8)

bag (4)
banana (3)
bank (R2)
bathroom (5)
bear (10P)
beard (3)
beautiful (5P)
because (7)
become (10P)
bed (4)
bedroom (5)
beer (8)
begin (7)
best (9P)
between (8P)
bicycle (6)
big (3)
billion (1)
birth (3)
biscuit (9)
black (3)
blackboard (4)
blender (10)
block (5P)
blood (4P)
blouse (4)
blue (3)
boat (8P)
body (4P)
book (1)
both (8P)
bottom (adj.2)
bowl (R3)
boy (3)
bread (9)

58

breakfast (5)
breakfast room (9)
bright (9P)
British (5)
brother (4)
brown (3)
build (5P)
building (7)
bus (7)
bus station (1)
Bushman (6P)
but (4)
buy (5)
by (7)

C
calculator (R3)
calendar (1)
call (v.6P)
camera (5)
cameraman (5)
campsite (6P)
can (v.3)
cape (6P)
capital (5P)
car (3)
card (9)
cardiologist (2P)
carefully (4P)
carpenter (4)
carrot (3)
carry (6P)
carve (8P)
cashier (10)
catch (v.8P)
cave (6P)
Celtic (7P)
centigrade (5P)
centimetre (3)
centre (10P)
ceremonial (7P)
ceremony (8P)
chair (1)
change (v.10)
characteristic (n./adj.7P)
cheap (3)
cheetah (8)

chess (6)
cheque (10)
chimpanzee (8)
choir (7P)
church (1)
cigarette (3)
cinema (1)
city (R1)
class (R2)
clean (v.5)
cleaner (10)
climate (10P)
clock (1)
close (4)
clothes (4P)
clothing (8P)
coal (10P)
coat (4)
coffee (1)
coffee pot (1)
cold (4)
colour (3)
come in (6)
comfortable (3)
common (8P)
commune (8P)
community (8P)
company (9)
complex (6P)
computer (3)
concert (7)
condition (5P)
connect (4P)
consent (v.8P)
contact (v.6P)
continent (10P)
control (v.8P)
cool (v.5)
cool (adj.4)
copper (10P)
corner (10)
cornflakes (8)
cost (v.10)
costume (7P)
cottage (9)
country (9)
crowd (5P)

culture (6P)
cup (1)
cupboard (1)
currency (10)
customer (5)

D
dairy (10P)
dark (3)
dear (2)
death (4P)
December (4)
deer (8)
dentist (3)
departure (7)
deposit (v.10)
deposit (n.10P)
desert (6P)
desk (1)
destination (7)
diagram (6)
dialect (6P)
different (7P)
difficult (4P)
dining room (5)
dinner (R2)
director (5)
disco (7)
diseased (4P)
dismantle (6P)
distance (9P)
do (v.5)
do (aux.5)
doctor (4)
does (aux.7)
dog (8)
dollar (8)
door (4)
double-decker (9P)
doughnut (9)
downtown (3P)
draw (6)
drawer (1)
dress (n.7P)
drink (v.8)
drink (n.9)
drive (6)

driving licence (6)
dry (4)
during (R3)
duty (10)

E
each (2)
earn (8)
east (2)
eat (5)
economic (6P)
efficient (9P)
egg (8)
eight (1)
eighteen (1)
eighty (1)
eleven (1)
engineer (4)
engineering (adj.9)
English (5)
Eskimo (8P)
especially (8)
estimate (8P)
every (9)
everything (8P)
exactly (6P)
examination (9P)
except (9P)
exciting (3P)
excuse (v.1)
exercise (n.8)
expensive (3)
expert (9P)
extensive (9P)
eye (3)

F
face (4P)
factory (5)
fahrenheit (5P)
fair (3)
family (4)
famous (3P)
fare (9P)
farm (8)
fast (3)
father (4)

fauna (10P)
February (4)
festival (7P)
fifteen (1)
fifty (1)
film (n.5)
find (v.5P)
fine (6)
finish (v.7)
first (5)
fish (n.8)
fish (v.8P)
five (1)
flat (5P)
flight (R2)
floor (1)
flower (6P)
fly (v.6)
food (8)
foot (3)
for example (3P)
foreign (6)
forest (8)
fork (2)
form (v.7P)
forty (1)
found (v.3P)
four (1)
fourteen (1)
French (5)
Friday (7)
from (3)
fruit (8)
fuel (9)
full (9P)
future (10P)

G
gallery (7)
gallon (9)
game (5P)
gather (6P)
generally (5P)
geography (2P)
German (6)
get up (8)
girl (3)

glass (2)
glasses (4)
glove (4P)
go (R2)
God (6P)
gold (10P)
golf (7)
good (4)
good afternoon (6
goodbye (6)
good evening (6)
good morning (6)
good night (6)
government (5P)
gown (7P)
grandfather (10)
grandmother (10)
green (3)
grey (3)
ground (adj.5)
group (6P)
guitar (6)

H
hair (3)
ham (8)
hand (4)
hard (adj.4P)
hat (4)
have (3)
have to (9P)
he (3)
heart (4P)
height (3)
hello (R1)
help (v.5)
her (poss.adj.3)
her (pro.5)
here (1)
hero (6P)
hey! (8)
hi! (6)
high (2P)
him (5)
his (4)
home (5)
homework (5)

horse (R3)
hospital (1)
hot (4)
hotel (1)
house (2P)
housewife (4)
housing (5P)
how (3)
however (10P)
hundred (1)
hunger (9)
hungry (9)
hunt (v.8P)
husband (4)
hut (6P)

I
I (3)
Iberian (7P)
ice (8P)
important (2P)
in (1)
in fact (8P)
in front of (2P)
inch (3)
increase (v.5P)
inside (9P)
instrument (4P)
interesting (10P)
iron ore (10P)
is (1)
island (3P)
it (1)
Italian (5)
its (3P)
ivory (8P)

J
January (4)
July (4)
June (4)
Just (a minute!) (5)
journey (9P)

K
kangaroo (R10)
kill (6P)

kilo (8)
kitchen (5)
knife (2)
knit (6)
know (8P)

L
lake (3P)
land (7P)
language (6)
large (7)
later (6)
latitude (8P)
law (7)
lawyer (8)
leaf (8)
leave (v.R2)
lecturer (3)
left (R1)
leg (8P)
lend (4)
let's (R2)
letter (5)
lettuce (3)
life (4P)
lighter (1)
like (adv.4)
listen (5)
little (6)
live (8)
living room (5)
loan (10)
local (6P)
loincloth (6P)
long (5)
look (v.3)
lunch (n.R3)
lung (4P)
luxury (9P)

M
machine (4P)
madam (1)
main (4P)
majority (10P)
make (5)
make-up (5)

man (3)
manager (10)
many (3P)
map (R1)
March (4)
marriage (8P)
marsupial (10P)
mask (4P)
maths (9)
matter (4P)
May (4)
may (aux.8P)
me (1)
meal (R3)
mean (10)
meat (8)
member (8P)
metre (2P)
Mexican (5)
middle (3P)
midnight (6)
midwest (2)
mile (5P)
million (1)
mine (R2)
mineral (10P)
minute (6)
mobile home (8)
model (3)
modern (4)
Monday (7)
money (R3)
month (3P)
most (6P)
motel (1)
mother (4)
move (v.5P)
much (4)
museum (7)
music (4)
musician (7P)
mutual (8P)
my (R1)

N
name (3)
national (9P)

near (1)
nearby (9P)
nearly (9P)
necessary (4P)
never (9)
new (5)
newspaper (8)
next (6)
night club (10)
nine (1)
nineteen (1)
ninety (1)
no (1)
nomadic (6P)
noon (6)
north (2)
not (1)
November (4)
now (5P)
number (7)
nurse (4P)

O
object (8P)
observe (5)
occasion (7P)
occupation (7P)
o'clock (6)
October (4)
of (3)
of course (3)
often (9)
OK (6)
old (2P)
on (1)
once (9)
one (1)
onion (3)
only (8P)
open (v.4)
open (adj.8)
opera singer (3)
operate (4P)
operation (4P)
opposite (2P)
orange (1)
ordinary (9P)

origin (7P)
other (6)
our (4)
ours (R2)
own (7P)

P
painting (6P)
pair (6P)
park (3P)
parking (9P)
part (3P)
particularly (10P)
party (10)
passport (7P)
past (6)
patient (4P)
pea (3)
pen (1)
pencil (3)
people (4P)
per (6)
perform (4P)
person (6)
personnel manager (5)
petrol station (1)
phone (10)
piano (6)
picnic (5P)
picture (3)
pie (9)
pipe (1)
place (3)
plan (6)
plane (6)
plastic (4P)
plate (2)
play (v.5)
please (1)
pleasure (4)
poet (7P)
poetry (7P)
poisoned (6P)
Polar (8P)
population (5P)
Portuguese (6)
postcard (1)

post office (1)
pound (2)
powerful (8P)
predict (5P)
prefer (10)
prepare (4P)
prevent (9P)
probably (8P)
problem (5P)
production (5)
property (6P)
provide (4P)
public (9P)
pull (v.8P)
puma (8)
pump (v.4P)
purchase (5)
put (2)
put on (5)

Q
quarter (6)
question (R3)
quickly (6)

R
racial (7P)
racing driver (3)
railway station (1)
rain (10P)
rainfall (4)
raise (8)
rapidly (5P)
read (5)
really? (3)
receive (10)
receptionist (8)
red (3)
reduce (9P)
refrigerator (10)
region (6P)
religion (6P)
rent (n.8)
replace (4P)
report (n.5)
reserves (10P)
respond (5)

restaurant (1)
rich (10P)
ride (6)
right (adj.1)
river (3P)
rock (6P)
rocky (8)
roof (9P)
root (6P)
round (adv.4P)
route (9P)
rush-hour (9P)

S
sail (v.8P)
salary (9)
salesman (3)
sales manager (4P)
same (4P)
sandwich (1)
Saturday (7)
saucer (2)
say (4)
school (R1)
schoolboy (R3)
schoolgirl (4)
Scottish (7P)
script (5)
seal (n.8P)
secondary (2P)
secretary (3)
see (3P)
September (4)
serious (5P)
seven (1)
seventeen (1)
seventy (1)
several (7P)
share (v.8P)
she (3)
sheep (8)
shelf (1)
shirt (4)
shoe (4)
shop (2P)
short (3)
shorthand (6)

shoulder (6P)
show (9P)
side (4P)
silver (10P)
similar (8P)
sing (5)
singer (3)
sir (1)
sister (4)
sit down (R3)
six (1)
sixteen (1)
sixty (1)
ski (6)
skin (6P)
sled (8P)
slim (3)
slow (3)
slowly (5P)
small (3)
smoke (v.8)
snow (8P)
society (8P)
soft drink (9)
solo (7P)
some (6P)
sometimes (10)
song (5)
sorry (5)
source (10P)
south (2)
space (9P)
Spanish (6)
speak (5)
special (4P)
spend (8)
spoon (2)
square (7)
star (5)
sterilize (4P)
stone (7)
stop (7)
stove (10)
straight (8P)
strange (10P)
street (R1)
student (3)

study (v.5)
suburb (8)
suburban (9P)
suitable (5P)
suitcase (8)
summer (5P)
Sunday (7)
supermarket (R3)
surgeon (4P)
surgery (4P)
surgical (4P)
sweep (10)
swim (6)
swimming-pool (9)
symbol (9P)
system (8P)

T
table (2)
take (6)
talk (5)
tall (3)
taxi driver (8)
tea (9)
teach (7)
team (8P)
telephone (1)
television (10)
temperate (10P)
temperature (4)
ten (1)
tennis (R2)
thank you (1)
that (1)
thatched (6P)
the (1)
theatre (9)
their (4)
theirs (R2)
them (5)
then (10)
there (adv.R2)
these (R1)
they (2)
thin (3)
thirst (9)
thirsty (9)

thirteen (1)
thirty (1)
this (1)
those (R1)
thousand (1)
three (1)
through (6P)
Thursday (7)
ticket (4)
time (6)
tired (4P)
toaster (10)
today (R2)
tomato (3)
tomorrow (7)
tonight (7)
too (2)
top (adj.2)
total (5P)
tower (7)
town (R1)
tradition (7P)
traditional (6P)
traffic (5P)
transport (9P)
trap (v.8P)
travel (7)
tree (9)
tribe (6P)
trip (4)
trousers (4)
truck (5P)
tube (9P)
Tuesday (7)
turf (8P)
TV (9)
twelve (1)
twenty (1)
twice (9)
two (1)
type (v.5)
typing (6)
typewriter (1)

U
umbrella (5)
unaverage (9)

uncomfortable (3)
under (4)
underground (5)
unit (8P)
university (R2)
unusual (10P)
uranium (10P)
us (R2)
use (v.9P)
usually (R2)

V
valley (7P)
valve (4P)
various (6P)
vary (9P)
vehicle (9P)
vein (4P)
very (3)
visit (v.5)
vivid (6P)
volleyball (8)

W
wait (v.R2)
wallaby (10P)
wander (6P)
warm (4)
wash (10)
washing machine (10)
watch (n.5)
water (9)
way (4P)
we (R1)
wear (4P)
weather (4)
Wednesday (7)
week (9)
weekend (8)
welcome (adj.1)
well (adv.6)
Welsh (7P)
west (2)
wet (4)
what (1)
when (4P)
where (1)

which (rel.pro.10P)
white (3)
who? (inter.pron.3)
whole (10P)
why (7)
wide (3P)
wife (4)
wild (6P)
will (aux.4)
window (4)
winter (5P)
with (3)
without (4P)
woman (3)
wood (8P)
work (v.4P)
work (n.7)
world (8P)
would (aux.9)
write (4)
writer (3)

Y
year (3)
yellow (3)
yellowish (6P)
yes (1)
you (1)
young (3)
your (R1)
yours (R1)

Z
zero (1)
zinc (10P)
zoo (3P)

Detailed notes for Pupil's Book 2

Unit one

This first unit introduces and provides practice of 'There is . . . . .' and 'There are . . . . .', that is, sentences in which 'there' is used to denote existence and not location (as in 'There is John'). The unit also provides opportunities for further practice of the present simple and other language first introduced in Pupil's Book One.

PRONUNCIATION MODELS

There's a restaurant in the Grand Hotel. /ðeəz ə ˈrestərɔːŋ in ðə ˈɡrænd houˌtel/

There are eighteen suites in the Tower Hotel. /ðeər ər ˈeitiːn ˈswiːts in ðə ˈtauə houˌtel/

Are there two theatres in Oxford? /ɑː ðeə ˈtuː ˌθiətəz in ˈɔksfəd/

There isn't an airport in Oxford. /ðeər ˈiznt ən ˈeəpɔːt in ˌɔksfəd/

Exercise one ⓣ
(B)

(Aural comprehension; introduction of 'There is . . . . .' and 'There are . . . . .')

Students may first need to be shown the spaces, some of which require numbers and others words.

The suggested sentences are:

1 There are two convention rooms in the Tower Hotel.
2 There are 300 double rooms in the Grand Hotel.
3 There are eighteen suites in the Tower Hotel.
4 There are two swimming pools in the Grand Hotel.
5 There are two restaurants in the Tower Hotel.

Note Students will need a little time to find the appropriate space and write in the necessary information. It may be necessary to repeat the sentences, which should be read at normal speed.

Exercise two ⓣ
(A)

(Aural comprehension practice and familiarization with the information to be used in oral practice)

The suggested sentences are:

1 There are twelve suites.	GH
2 There's a swimming pool in the hotel.	TH
3 There aren't any convention rooms.	GH
4 There isn't a bookstall in the hotel.	TH

5 There's a restaurant and a night club
   in the hotel.   GH

Exercise three
(C)

(Oral practice of 'There is . . . . .' and 'There are . . . . .'
in affirmative and negative sentences)
   In oral practice 'some' and 'any', which are introduced
in Unit Two, should be avoided. Students should notice
the difference between 'a' and 'one' (not two or more).
Negative sentences may be practised by contradiction:
Student 1 There are 400 rooms in the Grand Hotel.
Student 2 There aren't 400 rooms; there are 300. Etc.

Exercise four ⓣ
(D)

(Oral practice of 'yes/no' questions; 'Is there . . . . . ?',
'Are there . . . . .?' and the answers to these)
   When the answer to another student's question is 'No',
students should be encouraged to add to their answers:
No, there isn't, but there's a . . . . .
No, there aren't. There are (number).

Exercise five
(E)

(Writing practice of 'There is . . . . .' and 'There are . . . . .')
   The anticipated completions are:
a   There are _____ Grand
b   There is _____ (there are) two swimming
c   Is there _____ Grand; there is not
d   Is there _____ Tower; there is
e   Are there _____ Tower; there are
f   There is not a _____ in the _____ Hotel

Exercise six ⓣ
(A)

(Aural comprehension practice; familiarization with the
map)
   The suggested sentences are:
1   There is one college in Broad Street.   F
2   There are five museums in Oxford.   F
3   There are two theatres in Oxford.   T
4   There's a prison in Oxford.   T
5   There isn't a cinema in Oxford.   F

Exercise seven
(C)

(Further oral practice of 'There is . . . . .' and 'There
are . . . . .')
   This exercise provides an opportunity for plentiful
practice of both 'There is . . . . .' and 'There are . . . . .' in
affirmative and negative sentences since students can talk
about the whole city of Oxford and all the streets marked
on it.

Exercise eight ⓣ
(D)

(Further oral practice of 'Is there . . . . . ?' and 'Are
there . . . . . ?')

Once again students should be encouraged to provide further information after a 'No . . . . . ' answer. This activity can be extended into conversation about the students' own locality.

Exercise nine
(E)

(Further oral practice of 'There isn't . . . . . ?' and 'There aren't . . . . . '; contrast between 'There is a . . . . . in . . . . ' and 'The . . . . . is in . . . . . . ')
This exercise, too, can be extended to cover the locality, and provides a natural context for the negative.

Exercise ten
(E)

(Writing practice of 'There is . . . . . ' and 'There are . . . . .')
The anticipated completions are:

a There are
b There is
c Is there; there is
d is the; There is not
e Are there; there are
thirty-five

Exercise eleven ⊤
(F)
Dialogue 1

(Further oral practice of 'There is . . . . . ' and 'can'; introduction of containers)
A very similar dialogue can be practised first, involving objects only:
Student 1 Can I have a sandwich, please?
Student 2 Yes, there's one on that plate (over there). Etc.

Dialogue 2

(Further oral practice of 'There are . . . . . ' with 'Let's . . . . . ')
This dialogue involves the introduction of some other useful expressions: 'You're right' and 'What about . . . . . ?)
Note In both these dialogues it is important for students to understand clearly the distinction between existential 'there' and 'there' as adverb of position (deixis).

Exercise twelve
(D)

(Further oral practice of the present simple)
Students should study the chart carefully before being asked questions. Some teachers may wish to begin with some preliminary practice in the form of statements as students go through the information for the first time.
The exercise also provides a good opportunity for the revision of time expressions.
Students may be asked to do the activity in pairs or small groups, varying the kinds of questions they ask as much as possible.

Exercise thirteen
(E)

(Further writing practice of the present simple and various questions)

The anticipated completions are:
a do Bob and Jim; often have juice
b Does Mr Snell get up; does
c How do Bob and Jim go
d always gets up
e usually _____ at a quarter
f does Mrs Snell go; goes to

Exercise fourteen
(D)

(Further oral practice — conversation)
Conversation, which can be done in groups or pairs, can cover the whole daily routine and students should be encouraged to use as wide a range of questions in the present simple as possible. From time to time students will need a vocabulary item and should use the expressions learnt in Book One, Unit Five to ask for it.

Reading
comprehension ⓣ
(G)

A The answers are:

1	No	3	No	5	Yes	7	Yes
2	No	4	Yes	6	Yes	8	Yes

B The anticipated completions are:
1 large, modern passenger ship
2 2,000 passengers
3 three
4 Five (days)
5 large _____ comfortable

C The answers are:

1	T	3	F	5	T	7	T	9	F
2	F	4	F	6	F	8	F	10	T

D In this case, too, students are asked to transfer information from the passage to the interview. This can be given as homework or done in pairs in class.

Interaction
sequence ⓣ
(H)

(Introduction and practice of some ways of giving warnings)
This sort of interaction sequence provides an ideal opportunity for classroom drama involving action and humour. Short dialogues can be prepared in pairs. Students should look for ways of incorporating language from previous units in their mini-dramas. Later, pairs may be selected to perform their mini dramas at the front of the classroom.

Unit two

This unit deals with the distinction between countable and uncountable nouns, and the determiners (unit/mass), 'some' and 'any'. It also provides opportunities for the revision of 'have' and 'There is . . . . . ' and 'There are . . . . . ', as well as cumulative practice of 'can', the present progressive and the present simple.

PRONUNCIATION MODELS
They have some wire in their van. /ðei 'hæv səm 'waiər in ðeə `væn/
He doesn't have any switches. /hi: 'dʌzənt 'hæv eni `switʃiz/
Is there any milk in the kitchen? /is ðeər eni ˌmilk in ðə 'kitʃin/
How much flour do you need? /'hau 'mʌtʃ `flauə dju: ˌni:d/

Exercise one ①
(A)

(Introduction of new vocabulary and 'some' and 'any')
It will be noted that each van contains items in the singular, in the plural, and uncountable materials. Thus it is important for students to become quickly familiar with the new vocabulary through the illustration, etc.
The suggested sentences are:

1 Bob Small has some nails in his van.	T
2 The Temples have some wood.	F
3 Bob Small doesn't have any sockets in his van.	T
4 The Temples don't have any switches in their van.	F
5 The Temples don't have any wood in their van.	T
6 Bob Small doesn't have any wood in his van.	F
7 Bob Small has some sockets in his van.	F
8 The Temples have a ladder in their van.	T

Note 'Some' has two meanings and two corresponding phonetic forms: /sm/ means simply an indefinite quantity, whereas /sʌm/ means a certain quantity which is not large (e.g. I have some money but not enough). This unit is concerned only with the unstressed /sm/.

Exercise two
(C)

(Oral practice of 'some' and 'any' in contrast with 'a(n)'; further oral practice of 'have')
Some teachers may prefer to use 'has/have got' and

'hasn't/haven't got' instead of 'have' with 'do/does'. (See Book One, Unit Nine)

Exercise three
(D)

(Oral practice of 'any' in interrogative sentences, in contrast with 'a(n)')

This exercise can be made more communicative by getting some students to cover the illustration.

Note The problem of 'some' is not dealt with completely in this unit. It is possible to use 'some' in interrogative sentences when the orientation is positive. However, since the distinction between 'some' and 'any' in questions is a fine one, only 'any' should be used at this stage.

Exercise four
(E)

(Writing practice of 'some' and 'any' with 'have')

The anticipated completions are:

a has some
b do not have any
c Does _____ have an; does
d does not have a

e Do _____ have any;
    they do not
f have some
g does not have any

Exercise five Ⓣ
(A)

(Aural comprehension practice; familiarization with the recipes)

The suggested sentences are:

1 There's one cup of milk in the recipe.	AF
2 There are some almonds in the recipe.	AF
3 There isn't any milk in it.	OC
4 There's some salt in it.	BP
5 There are two teaspoonsful of baking powder in it.	OC
6 There are some breadcrumbs in it.	BP
7 There isn't any butter in it.	AF
8 There's some flour in the recipe.	OC
9 There are three eggs in the recipe.	BP
10 There's a cup of orange juice in it.	OC

Exercise six
(C)

(Further oral practice of 'some', 'any', 'there is' and 'there are')

Teachers may wish to begin this exercise by getting students to describe the kitchen and what there is in it systematically. This will allow problems of vocabulary and pronunciation to be dealt with.

Exercise seven Ⓣ
(D)

(Further oral practice of 'Is there . . . . . ?' and 'Are there . . . . . ?'; practice of the distinction between 'How much . . . . . ?' and 'How many . . . . . ?') A natural sequel to this exercise is the four-phase exchange:

Student 1 Is there any chicken soup in the kitchen?
Student 2 Yes, there is.
Student 1 How much is there? (How many tins are there?)
Student 2 Three (tins). Etc.
Note 'How many' can only be used with uncountable nouns if the containers are mentioned.

Exercise eight
(D)

(Further practice of 'How much . . . . . ?' and 'How many . . . . . ?')
    This activity, like the previous one, allows for plentiful practice of expressions of quantity. It can of course be extended to other recipes. In this case practice could begin with 'What do you need for (a) . . . . . ?'

Exercise nine
(D)

(Further practice of 'can'; practice of 'Why not?' and 'because')
    This exercise should be extended to cover other dishes known to the students.
Note Teachers may wish to follow up this series of exercises on 'some' and 'any' with some conversation practice:
a   about the locality or places known to the students: 'Are there any _____s in . . . . . ?' Etc.
b   about friends, family, etc.: 'Do you have any friends in . . . . . ?'

Exercise ten
(E)

(Writing practice of 'some', 'any' and new vocabulary)
    This exercise is in paragraph form and various completions are possible.

Exercise eleven

(Further writing practice: composition)
    This exercise should be prepared orally. Students in pairs can work out recipes (without specific quantities), asking the teacher for additional vocabulary as required. Then the paragraph can be written and read to the class.

Exercise twelve ⓣ
(F)

(Further oral practice)
    This activity provides an opportunity for varied further practice of several previously learnt items. Students should be encouraged to extend the list of foods available and to act out the dialogue at the front of the classroom after preparing it in groups or pairs.

Exercise thirteen
(E)
Dialogue 1

(Further writing practice)
    The anticipated completions are:
Do _____ any; do you want; How much

Dialogue 2	Can I; I want some; How much; have some; How many do you want; How much
Exercise fourteen **(D)**	(Further oral practice of 'can', the present simple and the present progressive) The drawings should only be used as a basis for the question in the present progressive, not for 'Can . . . . .?' questions. This activity can lead directly into the next.
Exercise fifteen	(Further oral practice: conversation) In preparation for this, students can be asked to fill out a chart similar to that in exercise 14, listing spare time activities and hobbies. Help will probably be needed with vocabulary.
Reading **comprehension** Ⓣ **(G)**	The answers are:

A

1	T	4	F	7	F
2	F	5	T	8	T
3	T	6	T	9	F

B

a	60 miles	e	two or three hundred passengers
b	twenty-two		
c	two and a half	f	about 40 minutes
d	English Channel		

C

a	T	e	F
b	T	f	F
c	F	g	F
d	T	h	F

D
  a In England (Ashington).
  b The one of Nat in front of the White House and the one of the vehicle.
  c Yes (they do).
  d The picture of the vehicle.
  e Yes (she is).
  f At 4.20 p.m.
  g Because of the expedition.

Interaction
sequence Ⓣ
(H)

(Introduction and practice of some ways of asking for the location of a service)
    Students will need help with the practice of the new vocabulary before being asked to change the dialogue. Practice can be extended by asking students to imagine they are in a certain place in the locality, and by extending the list of services.

Unit three

This unit provides practice both in the present progressive and the present simple. The way each is used to refer to present time is demonstrated, and in practice students are required to select the appropriate form. In this unit the present progressive is primarily used to refer to actions of 'limited duration' rather than actions actually in progress at the time of speaking (c.f. Book One, Unit Five).

Pronunciation Models are not given since no new forms are introduced.

Exercise one
(B)

(Reading comprehension: transfer of information)
The following is what students should write in the boxes from left to right:
designer _____ furniture and household equipment _____ furniture for a new hotel

Exercise two Ⓣ
(A)

(Aural comprehension and familiarization with the information to be used in oral practice)
The suggested sentences are:

1	Bob Croft works for an oil company.	T
2	Marion Laker is making a documentary about seals.	T
3	Bob Croft is building a canal in Nigeria.	F
4	Pauline Sharp manages a photographic studio.	T
5	Marion Laker works for a newspaper.	F
6	Frank Robinson is prospecting for oil.	F
7	Pauline Sharp is taking photographs for a travel book.	T
8	Frank Robinson is building a dam.	F
9	Bob Croft doesn't work for an engineering company.	T
10	Marion Laker makes films about children.	F

Exercise three
(C)

.(Further oral practice of the present simple in contrast with the present progressive)
Some teachers may wish students to have more practice in the formation of negative statements in these two tenses. This can be done by making incorrect statements.

Exercise four ⓣ
(D)

(Further oral practice of questions in the present simple and present progressive)
Some teachers may wish to include practice of 'yes/no' questions. This would make a longer sequence of questions and answers possible:

Student 1 Does Marion Laker design furniture?
Student 2 No, she doesn't.
Student 1 What does she do?
Student 1 She makes films about animals.
Student 1 Is she making a film about animals at present?
Student 2 Yes. She's making a documentary about seals in Canada. Etc.

Exercise five
(E)

(Writing practice of the present simple and present progressive)
The anticipated completions are:
a   a civil; builds
b   is building a canal in Nigeria
c   is _____ doing, She is taking photographs for a travel book
d   does Marion Laker

Exercise six
(C)

(Further oral practice of the present progressive)
In this exercise students should refer only to the three graphs for information. Negative sentences may also be practised.

Exercise seven
(C)

(Further oral practice of the present simple)
This exercise is based on the three tables. It can be treated as part of exercise 6 if desired.

Exercise eight
(C)

(Further oral practice of the present progressive)
In this case practice should focus on the six pictures.

Exercise nine
(D)

(Further oral practice of questions in the present simple and present progressive)
Many teachers will wish to omit exercises 6 to 8 and begin directly with question – answer practice. This can include many other questions: 'How many cars do they produce every year?', 'What is happening to exports?', 'What is the company building?' Etc.

Exercise ten ⓣ
(F)

(Further oral practice)
Although the first part of the dialogue cannot change much, the second part can be altered freely by changing the second question.

Exercise eleven **(E)**	(Further writing practice) The anticipated completions are: produces; make; is falling _____ are rising; export (sell) _____ import (buy) _____ make; export
Exercise twelve **(B)**	(Aural comprehension: transfer of information) The form should be completed with words and numerals and the graphs by continuing the line begun on each. The suggested passage is: The Sesma Company makes plastic tables and chairs. The company employs 280 people in its factory and 40 people in its offices. On average, it produces 28,000 tables and 170,000 chairs annually. At present sales are rising quickly but exports are falling a little. Production is increasing slowly.
Exercise thirteen Ⓣ **(F)**	(Further oral practice) This dialogue is designed to facilitate transfer into conversation among members of the class on similar topics. This is best done in pairs or groups.
Exercise fourteen **(C)**	(Further oral practice of the present simple) Some teachers may prefer to familiarize students with the information in the table via question – answer practice. However, it should quickly become possible for students to invent a short 'oral composition' of well connected sentences on any of the subjects.
Exercise fifteen Ⓣ **(F)**	(Further oral practice) This dialogue is intended to provide students with an opportunity of using the present simple and the present progressive together in a natural way. Students will need to hear several examples before understanding the full range of possibilities: the person asking can ask: 'Does Harry Roach work/live/have lunch/play . . . . . here?' The person answering should always begin 'Yes, but . . . . . ' and continue with any of the three possibilities not mentioned by the person asking.
Exercise sixteen **(E)**	(Further writing practice of the present simple and present progressive) The anticipated completions are: a has lunch b is playing bridge c Yvonne Finch having lunch d Arthur Brown live at

c does Susan Dale do
f live in York Crescent
g is playing chess at the

<table>
<tr><td rowspan="3">Reading
comprehension
(G)</td><td colspan="4">A The answers are:</td></tr>
</table>

Reading
comprehension
(G)

A The answers are:

a	T	c	F	e	T	g	T
b	F	d	F	f	F	h	F

B The answers are:

1	F	3	T	5	F	7	T
2	F	4	F	6	T	8	F

Interaction
sequence
(H)

(Introduction and practice of a way of complaining and a way of apologizing)
Note This sequence relates to Sequence Six in Book One.

First review and complementation unit

Exercise one

The following is a brief key to the exercises:

Practice of 'There is/are, any, How many . . . .' etc.)
a There are 45
b Are there any shelves; there are
c How many plates are there; There are
d There isn't a
e There are three
f How many footballs are there in the stock cupboard
g There is a
h Are there any ____ in room 2
i many ____ are there in; There is
j There are ____ tins of paint
k Are there any; there are not
l How many boxes of ____ are there; There are
m Are there any shelves; there are

Exercise two ⓣ

(Aural comprehension practice of 'there is/there are')
    The suggested text is:

There are 470 rooms in the Royal Hotel. They all have
a television and a shower, one double bed and two
armchairs. The Royal Hotel has 15 suites but the Super
Hotel has 45. There are two double beds in all the
rooms in the Super Hotel and three armchairs. There
are two swimming pools in the Royal Hotel and six
tennis courts; the Super Hotel has a swimming pool but
there aren't any tennis courts. There are two
restaurants and four bars in the Royal Hotel with three
shops in the entrance and parking outside. The Super
Hotel has a restaurant and three bars and a night club
but there aren't any shops and there is no parking. A
room in the Royal Hotel costs £25 a night, £5 more
than the Super Hotel.

Exercise three

(Practice of articles and pronouns: the /a/ an, it/they;
some/any)

1 The ____ a; It   4 A   7 any
2 The; They   5 any   8 some ____ the
3 a   6 an ____ the

78

Exercise four	(Further writing practice; composition) Encourage students to write short sentences, using 'and' 'or' 'but' where suitable.

Exercise five

(Practice of the present simple and the present progressive)

1	is not sleeping	6	Does your brother
2	does George do; plays		go; he does
3	am working	7	am listening
4	leaves	8	are waiting
5	is building	9	arrives
		10	are making

Exercise six

(Practice of the present simple and the present progressive) writes; travels; gets up; is having _____ is listening; plays _____ visits; is raining

Exercise seven

(Practice of some/any/a/an/+ nouns)

a	any water	e	any petrol	i	a stove
b	some tea	f	some oranges	j	a coffee pot
c	a typewriter	g	any eggs		
d	a cigarette	h	some paint		

Exercise eight

(Practice of be/have/can)

1	is	4	Have	7	Can
2	cannot	5	Is	8	are not
3	am	6	do you have	9	can; does not have
				10	Can; am

Exercise nine

(Vocabulary)

secretary	export	art school
film director	produce	supermarket
lecturer	import	technical college
civil engineer	sell	university
receptionist		music school
		post office
		newsagent
		tobacconist

flour	hammer
sugar	screw
butter	nail
pepper	electric saw
baking powder	insulating tape

Unit four

This unit introduces and provides practice of the infinitive with 'to' after certain verbs (like, want, learn, etc.) and with the semi-auxiliary 'have (got) to'. Thus the unit also provides further practice of the present simple. In addition there is an opportunity for revision of 'There is/ are . . . . .' and 'How much/many'.

PRONUNCIATION MODELS

Tony has to sleep in the daytime. /'touni 'hæz tə 'sli:p in ðə `deitaim/

Does she like to read novels ? /dʌz ʃi 'laik tə 'ri:d ˌnɔvəlz/

What does he want to do after school ? /'wɔt dəz hi 'wɔnt tə 'du: ɑ:ftə `sku:l/

Exercise one
(C)

(Introduction and practice of 'have to/has')
   Students should first read the short paragraphs and ensure that they understand them completely. A few comprehension questions can be asked, e.g. Where do they live? Can he sleep in the night? What time does she begin work? Etc. Some teachers may wish to combine this exercise with practice of 'can't':
   Student 1 The Snells can't go up the stairs: they have to use the elevator. Etc.

Exercise two
(D)

(Oral practice of 'have/has to'; further oral practice of 'why?' and 'because')
   This activity can be extended into personalized practice
   Student 1 What time do you get up in the morning?
   Student 2 At seven o'clock.
   Student 1 Why do you have to get up at seven? (so early)
   Student 2 Because I have to . . . . . Etc.

Exercise three
(E)

(Writing practice of 'have/has to')
   The anticipated completions are:
a   have to be
b   does Tony have to sleep
c   does Wendy have to stay; Because she has
d   Tony have to; he does

e   Mr and Mrs Watson have to; they do not
f   does Karen have to leave home; (has to) begin(s)

Exercise four ⓣ
(A)

(Aural comprehension practice; introduction of 'like to'
and 'want to')
The suggested sentences are:
1   This person likes to get up early.   P
2   This person wants to get married.   C
3   This person has to be home before 10 p.m.   C
4   This person doesn't want to go to university.   P
5   This person doesn't like to watch TV.   C

6   Peter wants to get married.   F
7   Carol likes to read novels.   T
8   Carol doesn't have to work in the garden.   T
9   Peter doesn't want to live with his parents.   F
10 Peter and Carol like to read novels.   T

Exercise five
(C)

(Oral practice of the infinitive with 'to' and 'like', 'want'
and 'has to')
Students may need a little help and guidance with the
questionnaire format and new vocabulary before
beginning this exercise. Negative statements involving the
same verbs may also be practised here.
Note 'Like' can also be followed by a verb in 'ing';
however, there is a slight change in implication. At this
stage students should practise only with 'to' and the
infinitive.

Exercise six ⓣ
(D)

(Further oral practice of the infinitive with 'to' and the
present simple)
There is an obvious opportunity for personalization
here: students may be asked to fill out a similar
questionnaire in their notebooks if they are of a suitable
age.
Alternatively, similar conversations can be held on
general likes, wishes and obligations.

Exercise seven
(E)

(Writing practice of the infinitive with 'to')
The anticipated completions are:
a   likes to
b   does Carol have; has to
c   Peter want to go; he does
d   Peter like to watch; he does
e   wants to _____ does not
f   Do Peter and Carol have; do
g   Does Carol like to; she does not
h   Does Carol have to be; she does

i Does Peter want; he does not
j Does Carol like; she does

Exercise eight Ⓣ
(F)

(Further oral practice)
    In this dialogue students are encouraged to use some common expressions involving the infinitive with 'to' and revise some previously learnt language in a natural everyday situation. This dialogue relates to Interaction Sequences 5 and 8 from Book One.
Note The infinitive can sometimes be omitted in the answer when the verb following 'to' is understood from the context, e.g. 'I'd like to'.

Exercise nine
(D)

(Cumulative oral practice)
    This activity provides an opportunity for practice of the infinitive with 'to' as well as practice of various previously learnt questions. If more information is needed to allow practice to be extended, students in pairs or groups can be invited to prepare other application forms modelled on that in the book and ask and answer questions about them.

Exercise ten
(D)

(Further oral practice of 'There is/are', 'How much/many . . . . . ?' and 'some/any')
    The inventory provided can be extended if desired, but a balance should be maintained between countable and uncountable nouns.

Exercise eleven
(E)

(Further writing practice)
    The anticipated completions are:

a are not any   d How many oranges are there
b How much flour is there   e Are there any; there are not
c Is there any rice/sugar   f Is there any; No, there is not

Reading
comprehension Ⓣ

(G)

The answers are:
A 1 Alabama   4 farms and prairies
   2 beautiful city   5 warm
   3 different from   6 in the East of the
                                      United States

B Massachusetts   9,399,317 square miles
    Connecticut   About 210 million
    Maine   Boston, New York, Washington D.C.
                               desert and mountain
    Texas   cold and windy
    Arizona

Michigan
Illinois
Wisconsin

C 1 five   4 study Indians   7 way of living
  2 in two days   5 a small   8 by car
  3 strongly built 6 in the jungle

**Interaction
sequence
(H)**

(Introduction and practice of one way of introducing
oneself over the telephone and stating what one is
telephoning about)
    In this and other telephone dialogues (c.f. exercise 8) it
is sometimes useful to bring 'toy' telephones into the
classroom in order to remind students of the kind of
communication they are simulating. Students may be
positioned so that they cannot see each other's faces in
order to show students how much more difficult
communication without eye contact can be.

Unit five

In this unit the possessive forms of singular and plural nouns are introduced. Thus the noun endings 's and s' and the new question word 'Whose . . . . . ?' are practised. The unit also offers practice of several previously taught question types, and of ordinals (first, second, twenty-seventh, etc.)

PRONUNCIATION MODELS

Mike is Alice's husband. /'maik iz 'ælisiz `hʌzbənd/
Mike's birthday is in March. /'maiks 'bə:θdei iz in `mɑ:tʃ/
Carol is Alan's wife. /`kærəl iz `ælənz `waif/
Jack is chairman of the Boys' Club. /'dʒæk iz 'tʃeəmən əv ðə 'boiz `klʌb/
Yvonne works for the children's fund. /i'vɔn 'wə:ks fə ðə `tʃildrənz ˌfʌnd/

Exercise one ⊤
(A)

(Introduction of the possessive form; familiarization with the family tree)
The suggested sentences are:

1	Carol Black is William Green's daughter.	T
2	Ronald's birthday is on July 16th.	T
3	Lorena is Alice Green's daughter.	F
4	William Green is Alan's father.	F
5	Mike and Alice Green are Tracy's parents.	T
6	Lorena is Carol Black's niece.	F
7	Mary Green is Alice Green's mother.	F
8	Alan Black is Ronald's uncle.	T
9	Mary's birthday is on June 7th.	F
10	Tracy Green is Lorena's cousin.	T

Exercise two
(D)

(Oral practice of the possessive form 's; introduction of 'When . . . . . ?')
This exercise also offers preliminary practice of some ordinals. This practice can be extended by getting students to ask and answer questions about their birthdays.

Exercise three
(C)

(Oral practice of family relationships and the possessive form)

This exercise introduces mainly a new set of vocabulary (but see Book One, Unit Four). Students will need some repetition practice of this before the exercise. Other relationships (mother-in-law, etc.) can be supplied if students wish to use them.

Note In all oral exercises on the possessive form, the distinction between the three possible ways of pronouncing 's will be important: /z/,/s/ and /iz/ (see pronunciation models).

Exercise four
(D)

(Further practice of the possessive form and of 'Who . . . . . ?')
This exercise can be done as part of the previous one. The 'Is . . . . . ?' question can also be practised:

Student 1 Is William Green Lorena's father?
Student 2 No, he isn't. He's her grandfather.
Student 1 Who is her father (, then)?
Student 2 Alan Black.

Exercise five
(E)

(Writing practice of the possessive form)
The anticipated completions are:
a Alan Black   e is Alice's birthday
b Ronald and Tracy are   f is Carol's
c is Lorena's   g Who is Carol's (Alan's)
d William is Tracy's (etc)

Exercise six ⓣ
(A)

(Aural comprehension; familiarization with the information to be used in oral practice)
Before beginning this exercise students should understand clearly the layout of the information about company employees and have read the information. Teachers may wish to begin with some simple comprehension questions (asked by students), such as: 'Who is the General Manager?', 'How many children does Jack have?' Etc.
The suggested sentences are:

1 George Scott's phone number is 05.   M
2 Pat Cook's office is on the second floor.   S
3 Sally Powell's hometown is Cardiff.   S
4 Sheila Church's son is called Henry.   M
5 Yvonne Finch's hobbies are cooking
  and stamp-collecting.   S

6 Charles is Pat Cook's husband.   F
7 Jack Kirby's hobbies are reading and singing.   F
8 Pat Cook is a member of the Ladies' Committee.   T
9 Sally Powell's office is on the second floor.   F
10 Sharon is George Scott's daughter.   T

Exercise seven
(C)

(Further oral practice of 's; oral practice of the possessive form of plural nouns)

Three differently written possessive endings are practised (singular noun + apostrophe s, plural nouns + apostrophe and irregular plural nouns + apostrophe s).

Exercise eight ①
(D)

(Further oral practice of the possessive and some questions)

This exercise can be expanded into personalized practice by getting three or four students to provide similar data to that in the company newspaper on the board. If this is done, it may be helpful to choose students whose names have different endings to allow for the distinction between /s/,/z/ and /iz/ in the possessive form. (Voiceless consonants in the name ending will give /s/ in the possessive, a vowel or a voiced consonant will give /z/ and an 's' or 'z' etc. sound of any sort will give /iz/.)

Exercise nine
(E)

(Writing practice of the possessive forms)

Since the only difference between possessive forms after singular, plural nouns and an irregular plural is in the written form, it is important to emphasize the differences in this exercise, and perhaps refer to the grammar summary at this stage.

The anticipated completions are:

a Manager's office is on
b the Sales Manager's
c George Scott's hometown
d the Production Manager's
e Powell's phone
f Yvonne Finch's
g Ladies' Committee
h Boys' Club
i of the Music Lovers' group
j He is Sheila Church's husband

Exercise ten
(D)

(Further practice of the possessive form and 'like to'; introduction of 'Whose . . . . . ?')

Some teachers may wish to begin the exercise with some further practice of 'there is' and 'there are', by getting students to describe every detail of the illustration.

Exercise eleven
(D)

(Further oral practice of the possessive form, 'Whose . . . . . ?' and 'like to')

It may be easier to begin by asking students to write down the names of their favourite singer, writer, filmstar (actor, actress), composer, etc. This will encourage students to respond more readily when they are talking in groups or pairs. If students wish to ask the follow-up question 'Why?', this should be encouraged but help may be needed with the answer.

Exercise twelve ⓣ
(F)

(Further oral practice of 'Whose . . . . . ?' and other questions)
This can be practised realistically in the classroom by collecting students' books, pens, bags, etc. together at the front of the classroom and asking a student to give them back to their owners by asking and answering questions.

Exercise thirteen
(D)

(Further oral practice of 'Whose . . . . . ?')
This can be extended by bringing magazine pictures into the class.

Exercise fourteen
(E)

(Further writing practice)
The anticipated completions are:
a Carlos Vergara's _____ under
b does she have; Her boyfriend's
c Whose books does she
d Whose _____ does she, Bert Starr's
e Whose; It is
f Whose skirt do

Exercise fifteen
(D)

(Further oral practice: cumulative)
This exercise is designed to stimulate oral composition: after a short while students should be able to say several consecutive sentences about any of the people mentioned in the company newspaper.

Exercise sixteen

(Further writing practice: composition)
This should follow on naturally from exercise 15 and may be done for homework, after a specimen has been worked out collectively on the board.

Reading comprehension ⓣ
(C)

The answers are:

A	1	F	3	F	5	F	7	F
	2	T	4	F	6	T	8	T

B a not warm   d after breakfast
   b a lot of wind   e noisy
   c near Hamilton   f in Canada
                          g dirty
                          h beside the lake

Interaction sequence ⓣ
(H)

(Introduction and practice of 'Shall I . . . . . ?')
Practice of this interaction sequence could be combined with revision of 'Will you . . . . . ?' — Sequence Two of Book One.
The answers are:
A 1 + Bd   A 2 + Ba   A 3 + Bc   A 4 + Bb

Unit six

In this unit several new prepositions are introduced:
Prepositions of location or direction: across, along, through, past, over, up, down, beside, between, from, to.
Prepositions of time: before, after, between, from, to.
In addition, previously taught prepositions are revised, and the present simple and the possessive forms are practised further.
Pronunciation models are not given because it would not be feasible to cover all new items.

Exercise one ⑦
(B)

(Aural comprehension practice of prepositions of direction)
Students should be made familiar with the new vocabulary in the key and how it applies to the illustration before beginning the exercise.
Students should fill in the names in pencil first (in small writing).
The suggested sentences are:
1 John is walking over the bridge.
2 Fred is walking through the gate.
3 Jack is swimming under the bridge.
4 Jim is walking past the house.
5 Ted is walking along the road.
6 Bill is swimming across the river.
7 Mike is walking from the house to the church.
8 Bob is walking up the hill.
9 Peter is walking through the wood.
10 Joe is walking across the road.
11 Harry is walking across the river.
12 Frank is walking from the church to the wood.
13 George is walking down the hill.
14 Alan is walking along the river.

Exercise two
(D)

(Oral practice of new prepositions; further practice of the present progressive)
Students should first make sure that their answers to exercise 1 are right. Then this exercise can be turned into a game: students look at their books for one minute then close them. Teams take it in turns to answer questions

from students in other teams. Each correct answer wins a point.

Note Some students may need further help with the exact meaning of some of the prepositions. Help can be given by means of arrow drawings on the board (see Grammar Section).

Exercise three ⓣ
(B)

(Aural comprehension practice: prepositions of location and 'There is/are')

Let the students first copy a larger version of the picture in the Pupil's Book into their notebooks, and then draw the items on their own picture.

Students should be given sufficient time between sentences to draw the objects.

The suggested sentences are:

1 There's an umbrella on the chair.
2 There are some shoes on the chair.
3 There are some bags under the table.
4 There's a book in the drawer.
5 There's a picture between the window and the door.
6 There are some apples in the box.
7 There's a big plate on the table.
8 There are some sandwiches on the plate.
9 There's a clock on the wall on the left.
10 There are some bananas on the floor beside the box.

Exercise four
(D)

(Aural practice of prepositions of location and 'There is/are')

This practice can be supplemented by work with other drawings or wallcharts containing similar objects and furniture.

Exercise five ⓣ
(A)

(Aural comprehension and familiarization with the information to be used in oral practice)

Before beginning this exercise students will need to be quite familiar with the contents of the reading passage and tables. Study of these can be set as homework, and problems of vocabulary dealt with before the exercise. A fairly large map of England would be useful in this and the succeeding three exercises.

The suggested sentences are:

1 The tour goes through Bradford.   2
2 The tour leaves at a quarter to eight.   2
3 The tour returns at about twelve o'clock.   3
4 On this tour, visitors can go up a tower.   1
5 On this tour, visitors can go to the theatre.   3

6	Tour One departs from Kendal.	T
7	Tour One goes through the Ure Valley.	F
8	Tour Two stops for lunch at the Red Lion.	F
9	On Tour Three, visitors can go round Warwick Castle.	T
10	On Tour Two, visitors can visit Wordsworth's cottage.	F

Exercise six (C)

(Further oral practice of prepositions and present simple)
Teachers may prefer students to concentrate their description and deal with one tour at a time.

Exercise seven Ⓣ (D)

(Further oral practice of prepositions and the present simple, interrogative)
Teachers may wish most students to close their books and to reconstruct the tours in tabular form or on sketch maps by asking the questions of a group of students who have their books open.

Exercise eight (E)

(Writing practice of the present simple and prepositions)
The anticipated completions are:

a	returns to Leeds	e	leaves at ____ on
b	stops at the ____ for	f	goes through
c	go past	g	goes through ____ to
d	on; go round Warwick Castle	h	Before ____ on ____ in

Exercise nine Ⓣ (F)

(Further oral practice)
In this dialogue students are able to practise several of the prepositions in a natural context together with several previously learnt items. (Can I help you?, I want . . . . . Etc.)
The dialogue should of course be adapted to refer to possible tours in the students' locality (cf. exercise 10)

Exercise ten

(Further writing practice: composition)
Students will probably find this easier if some suggestions are given and if they are able to work in pairs or groups. Before doing the guided composition, representatives should be invited to talk about the tours they have invented.

Exercise eleven (D)

(Further oral practice of the possessive form and 'Whose . . . . . ?')
Several other questions may also be practised: e.g. Is Carol's sweater in . . . .?, How many shirts are there in the . . . . . Etc.

Reading	The answers are:

Reading	The answers are:

Reading
comprehension Ⓣ
(G)

The answers are:

A	1	F	3	T	5	F	7	T
	2	F	4	T	6	F	8	F

B	1	E	3	D	5	B
	2	F	4	A	6	C

Interaction
sequence Ⓣ
(H)

(Introduction and practice of some expressions for asking the way and for giving directions)

This sequence relates to Sequence Two in Unit Two.

Every opportunity should be taken of extending practice by relating it to the locality of the classroom or to other large street plans that are available.

Note In order for students to be able to use 'left' and 'right' meaningfully, it is important to give the speakers a precise position.

Second review and complementation unit

The following is a brief key to the exercises:

Exercise one

(Practice of prepositions)
from _____ at _____ on; past _____ through; over _____
under _____ up; for _____ at; beside (near); After _____
through _____ down; In _____ at; in _____ up; _____ round
(around); across _____ to _____ for _____ at; After _____ to;
on _____ on; to _____ between

Exercise two

(Practice of the present simple in the interrogative form)
1 Does the train stop at   4 Does the train go
2 What time does the train   5 What time does the train
3 Where does the train stop   return

Exercise three

(More practice on prepositions)

1 in	4 on	7 beside
2 to	5 past	8 up
3 along	6 at	9 across
		10 on _____ through

Exercise four

(Practice of the possessive forms)

1 Anne's dog	4 The Browns' house	7 The Browns' car
2 Jill's trousers	5 Anne's hair	8 Jill's bag (The
3 Jill's dog	6 Jill's dog	Browns' house, etc.
		9 Jill's bag
		10 Mary's cats

Exercise five

Vocabulary

across	**valley**	**fishing**
along	mountain	cooking
down	lake	gardening
through	river	photography
stadium	**coat**	**libary**
tennis court	jacket	police station
swimming pool	hat	Town Hall
football field	blouse	tourist office

Exercise six ⓣ   In this exercise students will need time to write a name or words in the spaces provided.

The suggested sentences for reading are:

1 Mr Croft is 42 years old.
2 Miss Laker's house is white.
3 Mr Small is 38 years old. He's an engineer.
4 The Smiths' house is green. Their car is a Rover.
5 Miss Laker is a film director.
6 Mr Small's house is number 35.
7 Mr Croft's house is blue.
8 Miss Laker's car is a Datsun.
9 Mr Croft's house is number 31.
10 The Smiths are photographers.

Exercise seven
1 Mr Small's   5 house
2 Mr Croft's   6 a film director;
3 Miss Laker's _____   Her house is
   Mr Small's   7 The Smiths' car
4 His car   8 Whose house is

Exercise eight   This exercise may be prepared by giving a model on the board.

Exercise nine   (Practice of word order)

1 Where does the tour stop for lunch?
2 Whose pen are you using?
3 Why does Frank have to wear a uniform?
4 What time does the flight leave?
5 What is Jack doing at the moment?
6 Whose dress do you prefer?
7 Do you want to go to university after secondary school?
8 Does Alfred work for an oil company?

Exercise ten   (Practice of the present simple, present progressive, infinitive with 'to')

1 writing   6 buy____ to go/drive
2 to watch   7 put
3 read   8 listening
4 go   9 drive; to drive; to take
5 to play   10 to have; writing

Exercise eleven   (Practice of question forms)

A What; Whose; Where; Do; Why; What
B What time; Can; How much; How many

Unit seven

This is the first of a series of three units on the past simple tense. This unit is concerned only with the past tense of 'be', 'was' and 'were', used as main verbs. These forms are practised in all the sentence patterns students have learnt to associate with 'be': subject + 'be' + complement, subject + 'be' + prepositional phrase, 'There is/are' + noun + prepositional phrase, etc. The unit also offers revision practice of 'is' and 'are' for contrast.

PRONUNCIATION MODELS

They were famous engineers. /ðei wə ˈfeiməs endʒiˋniəz/
She was a dancer. /ʃi wɔz ə ˋdɑːnsə/
How old was he? /hau ˋould wɔz hi/
Were they married in 1970? /wɔː ðəi ˈmærid in ˌnaintiːn ˈsevənti/
There wasn't a school in Gravestone. /ðeə ˈwɔzənt ə ˋskuːl in ˌgreivstoun/
Were there any saloons? /wɔː ðeər eni səˌluːnz/

Exercise one
(C)

(Introduction of oral practice of 'was' and 'were')
Teachers may wish to add to the list of well-known people particularly by making reference to the students' knowledge. This exercise also offers practice of some vocabulary related to professions and adjectives of nationality.
Note: The weak forms /wəz/ and /wə/ will need special practice.

Exercise two
(D)

(Oral practice of 'was' and 'were' in questions)
Some teachers may prefer the question 'What nationality was he?' to 'Where was he from?'. This exercise also allows for practice of the 'yes/no' questions: 'Was Chaplin American?' etc. and of the short answers 'Yes, he was' and 'No, he wasn't' etc.

Exercise three
(D)

(Further oral practice of 'was' and 'were' and some adjectives)
Nearly all the adjectives in this group will be new to the students. They should be clarified by example and practised carefully before students are asked to use them.

Students should be asked to find appropriate adjectives for any other famous people of the past who have been mentioned. The adjectives can be applied to the famous people mentioned in the book in the following way: 'clever' and 'talented' can be used for all (with the possible exception of Cortes and Pizarro), 'brave' should be used mainly of Cortes and Pizarro and the Wright Brothers, 'eccentric' of Gauguin, 'strong' of Cortes and Pizarro, 'amusing' of Chaplin, and 'graceful' and 'beautiful' of Mata Hari.

Exercise four
(E)

(Writing practice of 'was' and 'were')
The anticipated completions are:

1 was	5 were Orville and Wilbur
2 was; was	Wright from; were
3 were the Bachs	6 Was Gauguin a; was not; was
4 was Mata Hari like; was	

Exercise five ⓣ
(A)

(Aural comprehension; practice in distinguishing past from present; familiarization with the information to be used in oral practice)
It is particularly important that these sentences should be read with normal stress and at normal speed.
The suggested sentences are:

1 Pauline Fry's a teacher.	PR
2 Jim's hair was long.	PA
3 Peter and Pauline weren't married.	PA
4 George and Mary're married.	PR
5 Karen was fat.	PA
6 Peter's a Bank Manager.	PR
7 Pauline and Jim aren't students.	PR
8 Mary Scott was a secretary.	PA

Exercise six
(C)

(Further oral practice of 'was' and 'were' in contrast with 'is' and 'are')
This exercise also provides an opportunity for practice of negative statements with 'wasn't' and 'weren't': e.g. Peter is a Bank Manager now, but in 1970 he wasn't a Bank Manager; he was a cashier.

Exercise seven ⓣ
(D)

(Further oral practice of interrogative sentences with 'was' and 'were')
Practice can be extended by getting students to talk about themselves four or five (or more) years ago. It may be helpful to begin by selecting a year and asking students to fill out the same sort of information as appears in the table about the 'Albion Bowling Team', for themselves or,

by asking questions about the two or three people in their group.

Exercise eight ⊤
(D)

(Further oral practice)
As a 'research' project, students can be asked to find out a little about the past of their favourite singers, actors, sports personalities, etc. for homework. This exercise can then be extended into conversation about these and other important people that the teacher selects.

Exercise nine
(E)

(Further writing practice of 'was', 'were', 'is' and 'are')
The anticipated completions are:
1 was _____ she is a housewife
2 were single/were not married
3 Were; they were
4 was Peter's; He was
5 were; was 39 _____ was 37
6 Jim's hair was _____ he was
7 Was Jim married; was
8 was Pauline; was

Exercise ten
(D)

(Further oral practice of questions with 'were')
This kind of exercise can also be done with other sporting events, e.g. the World Cup (was), the Pan American Games (were), etc.
Note It is important that students should be able to distinguish clearly between 'where'/weə/ and 'were'/ wə:/.

Exercise eleven
(D)

(Further oral practice of questions with 'was' and the possessive form)
This exercise also provides an opportunity for practising questions beginning with 'Was . . . . . ?' and the short answers 'Yes, it was' and 'No, it wasn't'.

Exercise twelve
(E)

(Further writing practice of 'was')
The anticipated completions are:
1 was at
2 was Sir Walter's lunch
3 was Sir Walter's meeting with the Ministers
4 Where was his interview with the press
5 Was Sir Walter's speech
6 What time were his

Exercise thirteen
(C)

(Oral practice of 'There was' and 'There were')
This exercise contains some new vocabulary which will need to be introduced and practised at the beginning of the exercise.

Exercise fourteen **(D)**	(Oral practice of 'There was/were' in questions) This exercise can be extended to conversation about changes in the students' locality.

Reading comprehension ⓣ **(G)**

The answers are:

A a F   c T   e F   g F
   b T   d T   f T   h F

B Some examples of questions and answers are provided on the tape.

C 1 a postcard   4 difficult
   2 Arizona and Colorado 5 Spanish
   3 Nayarit   6 several days

Interaction sequence ⓣ **(H)**

(Introduction and practice of a way of making suggestions)
The answers are:
1 c   3 d   5 e
2 a   4 b

Students may enjoy inventing problems and asking others to help by making suggestions. They may need help with extra vocabulary.

Unit eight

This second unit on the past tense introduces the past tense form of several regular and irregular verbs and the question 'What happened . . . . . ?', together with several time expressions for referring to past time ('last . . . . .', '. . . . . ago' etc). The use of the auxiliary 'did' in negative statements and interrogatives is not practised until Unit Nine.

PRONUNCIATION MODELS

He invented the printing press. /hi in'ventid ðə `printiŋ ˌpres/
They discovered America. /ðei dis'kʌvəd ə`merikə/
He finished the Sistine Chapel in 1512. /hi 'finiʃt ðə 'sistiːn 'tʃæpl in 'fiftiːn `twelv/
What happened in 1517? /wɔt 'hæpənd in 'fiftiːn sevən`tiːn/
Luther began the Reformation. /'luːθə bi'gæn ðə refə`meiʃn/

Exercise one

(Familiarization with the information to be used in oral practice)

The short reading passage can be treated as reading comprehension. Most students will have no trouble completing the model sentences with the appropriate past tense form once difficulties of vocabulary have been clarified since most of the events chosen are well known: Gutenberg invented . . . . . ; Leonardo painted . . . . . ; Henry VIII became . . . . . ; Michelangelo finished . . . . . ; Machiavelli wrote . . . . .; Luther began . . . . .

Exercise two
(C)

(Oral practice of several past tense forms and dates)

Before beginning this exercise students may need some repetition practice of the past tense forms. Teachers may wish to print out the varying pronunciation of the 'ed' ending of regular verbs: /d/ after a voiced consonant or vowel, /t/ after a voiceless consonant and /id/ after 't' or 'd'.

Exercise three
(D)

(Oral practice of 'What happened . . . . .?' and past tense forms.)

This can be made more communicative by asking students to close their books. Teachers and students may enjoy talking about other events, involving the same verbs, which are important in history. After some research at home students can test each other's general knowledge. The expression 'I don't know' will be useful here.

Exercise four (E)

(Writing practice of some past tense forms and 'What happened . . . . .?')

The anticipated completions are:

a invented
b went
c discovered America
d happened; Michelangelo finished
e Leonardo painted
f happened in 1517; began the Reformation
g Henry VIII became King of England

Exercise five Ⓣ (B)

(Aural comprehension, especially of numbers; familiarization with information to be used in oral practice)

After each sentence students should be given some time to write the appropriate number in the appropriate space in pencil.

The suggested sentences are:

1 Last year the government gave thirty million dollars to farmers.
2 The government lent ninety million dollars to the universities last year.
3 The government spent six hundred million dollars on health last year.
4 In 1976 the government built a hundred and fifteen schools.
5 In 1966 they built only thirteen hospitals and trained three hundred and eighteen doctors.
6 Last year the government built a hundred and seventy thousand houses.
7 In 1976 they trained three thousand two hundred nurses.
8 Last year they trained six thousand school teachers.
9 In 1976 the government employed seventy eight thousand men.
10 In 1966 the government employed forty five thousand women.
11 Last year a litre of milk cost forty five cents.
12 In 1976 a gallon of petrol cost two dollars thirty.
13 In 1966 a hundred grams of butter cost forty cents and a loaf of bread cost sixteen cents.

Note It is very important that students should understand the layout and subject matter of this fictional financial report before beginning the exercise, and that afterwards the answers are checked by putting the correct ones on the board, or by showing students an enlarged copy in which all spaces are filled.

Exercise six Ⓣ
(A)

(Aural comprehension and familiarization with the information to be used in oral practice)
The suggested sentences are:

1	Last year the government lent thirty million dollars to farmers.	F
2	In 1976 a litre of milk cost thirty cents.	T
3	Last year the government employed eight thousand four hundred and fifty men.	F
4	In 1966 the government built thirteen hospitals and ninety-eight schools.	T
5	In 1966 a litre of milk cost fifteen cents and a loaf of bread sixteen cents.	T
6	Last year the government spent sixty million dollars on industry.	F
7	Last year the government built two hundred and seventy schools and a hundred and seventeen thousand houses.	F
8	In 1966 the government employed forty-six thousand men and forty-five thousand women.	T
9	Last year a gallon of petrol cost three dollars.	T
10	In 1976 the government built a hundred and fifty schools.	F

Note There is some emphasis in both these aural comprehension exercises on the distinction between, for example, 'sixty' where the stress is on the first syllable, and 'sixteen' where the stress is on the second syllable (or sometimes on both syllables). Some teachers may wish to take advantage of these exercises for general revision of numbers.

Exercise seven
(C)

(Oral practice of some past tense forms and numbers)
This exercise can be extended if real financial reports containing similar information are available.

Exercise eight
(E)

(Writing practice of some past tense forms)
The anticipated completions are:

1 spent	5 trained 2,500
2 lent ____ to	6 lent 100 million

3 employed	7 built 24
4 cost 30 cents	8 cost 55 cents

Exercise nine

(Reading comprehension: transfer of information)
The answers are:
Paris, France; 3 weeks, 1975; Versailles, Montmartre, the Eiffel Tower; Notre Dame, the Louvre, etc.

Exercise ten
(C)

(Oral and writing practice of more past tense forms)
This exercise can develop into oral composition in which students produce series of connected sentences similar to the paragraph about Tracey. Then students can do a short written composition on similar lines.

Exercise eleven

(Further oral and writing practice)
Students should be given five minutes or so to work out what they are going to say and to ask questions about vocabulary they may need before being asked to talk to the class. This can then be written for homework.

Exercise twelve Ⓣ
(F)

(Further oral practice)
This dialogue can develop into the game of Alibi: students in groups of two or three plan their alibi for a crime, selected by the teacher, committed on the previous evening. The alibi should be a collective one and contain a sequence of at least four events with times and places. The students then take it in turns to tell their group's story while the other members of the group wait outside the classroom. The students listening note any differences in the versions and decide whether the group is guilty.

Note Teachers may wish to use this activity to begin introducing questions with 'did'; alternatively the activity can be done again towards the end of Unit Nine.

Exercise thirteen
(C)

(Oral practice of more past tense forms and the months)
Students can prepare for this exercise in pairs or groups after the new vocabulary has been introduced by means of mime, drawing, etc.

Note Any doubts about the story should be clarified by the answers to exercise 15, given below.

Exercise fourteen
(D)

(Further oral practice of past tense forms and 'What happened . . . . .?')
This can be made more communicative if students are asked to close their books or cover the pictures.

Exercise fifteen
(E)

(Writing practice of some past tense forms)
The anticipated completions are:
sold; In _____ bought _____ planted _____ in; lent _____
flew to; climbed a mountain _____ fell _____ broke; was
_____ in _____ went; met _____ on; visited _____ got
married; returned _____ fell _____ broke; had

Exercise sixteen

(Further oral practice)
This conversation exercise is designed to encourage
students to relate the past tense forms they have learnt in
this unit to their own experience. However, it is likely
that some students will need more vocabulary which can
be provided during a preliminary period of three or four
minutes in which students remember and write down the
important events of their last year.

Reading
comprehension ⓣ
(G)

The answers are:

A	1 F	3 A	5 H	7 D
	2 G	4 C	6 B	8 E

B 1 hot   4 before everybody
  2 before 1500AD   5 large
  3 a number of cities 6 Some of

Interaction
sequence ⓣ
(H)

(Introduction and practice of one way of asking for and
giving opinions)
Practice of these expressions can be stimulated by
asking each student to write down the name of one actor/
actress, one city, one dish, etc. before the activity begins.
Practice can then develop in changing pairs: students all
stand and move naturally from one person or group to
another. This may also provide an opportuntity for
further practice of introductions and apologies, etc.

Unit nine

In this unit, the auxiliary 'did' is introduced and practice
of negative statements, various kinds of questions and
short answers in the past tense is offered. There is also
practice of the infinitive of purpose and contrast of the
past tense with the present simple.

PRONUNCIATION MODELS

When did they go to the moon ? /ˈwen did ðei ˈgou tə ðə
ˈmuːn/

What did Alcock and Brown do in 1919 ? /ˈwɔt did ˈɔːlkɔk
ən ˈbraun ˈduː in ˈnaintiːn nainˈtiːn/

Who phoned the police ? Linda did. /ˈhu: ˈfound ðə pəˈliːs
ˈlində did/

Did the thieves make a noise ? Yes, they did. /did ðə ˈθiːvz
ˈmeik əˌnoiz ˈjes ðeiˈdid/

He went there to repair a television. /hi ˈwent ðeə tə riˈpeər
ə ˈteliviʒn/

Exercise one ⓣ
(A)

(Aural comprehension practice; familiarization with the
information to be used in oral practice)

Before beginning the exercise students should read the
short paragraph. Any difficulties with the vocabulary can
also be dealt with before the exercise.

The suggested sentences are:

1 Yuri Gagarin walked on the moon.	N
2 Alcock and Brown flew across the Atlantic in 1919.	Y
3 Did Amundsen reach the South Pole in 1911?	Y
4 Did Aldrin and Armstrong make the first space flight?	N
5 Did Christian Barnard transplant a human heart in 1957?	N
6 Did Gagarin make the first space flight in 1961?	Y
7 Did Hillary and Tensing reach the top of Mount Everest in 1935?	N
8 Did Armstrong walk on the moon?	Y

Exercise two (C)	(Further oral practice of some past tense forms and dates, and of 'didn't')

This exercise provides a good opportunity to introduce negative statements in the past tense. This can be done by asking students to deny incorrect statements:

Student 1 Barnard transplanted a human heart in 1957.

Student 2 He didn't transplant a human heart in 1957: he did it in 1967. Etc.

Teachers may wish to return to the famous events of the Renaissance in Unit Eight and continue practice of the negative with these.

Note Teachers may wish also to practise 'ago' as an alternative to the various dates.

Exercise three ⓣ
(D)

(Oral practice of questions in the past tense, with 'did')

Teachers may wish to extend this practice by adding to the list of famous achievements or by referring students to the history of countries they are familiar with. After research at home students may enjoy testing each other's general knowledge in a quiz. The famous people on page 69 of the Pupil's Book can also be used in this exercise. Some examples are provided on the tape.

Exercise four
(E)

(Writing practice of questions in the past tense)

The anticipated completions are:

a did
b did _____ transplant a human heart
c Amundsen reach; he did not
d did; reached the top of Mount Everest
e make the first space flight
f Did Aldrin and Armstrong walk; did

Exercise five ⓣ
(A)

(Aural comprehension practice; familiarization with the picture story)

Students should look carefully at the pictures (at home) before beginning the exercise. They should understand clearly that the various series of pictures deal with different characters in chronological sequence, and that the merging together of the three lines of pictures into two, and then one, symbolizes the coming together of the characters.

The suggested sentences are:

1 Linda phoned the doctor.	B3
2 Doug and Dinsdale left prison.	A1
3 George heard a noise next door.	A4
4 Mary went to bed.	B2

5	Doug and Dinsdale bought some tools.	A3
6	Linda and George saw a terrible film.	C1
7	The doctor hit Doug.	A5
8	The thieves saw an empty house.	A2

Exercise six
(C)

(Further oral practice of the past tense, affirmative and negative)

This exercise can be treated as an oral composition: a student begins the story and says two or three connected sentences, then another continues. When the end of the story is reached the process can be repeated more than once to ensure that all students have a chance to practise it, and that everyone understands the story.

Note In the oral composition every opportunity should be taken of using appropriate connecting words ('and', 'but', 'so', 'then', etc.)

Exercise seven ⓣ
(D)

(Further oral practice of various questions in the past tense; further practice of 'Why . . . . . ?' and 'because')

A clock or time reference is provided with each picture to allow for plentiful practice of 'When . . . . . ?' and 'What time . . . . . ?'. Students should be encouraged to ask questions in logical sequence rather than haphazardly, but also to vary the kind of question frequently. Further practice of this kind can be obtained by referring back to one of the reading comprehension passages in the past tense.

Exercise eight
(F)

(Further oral and writing practice)

Students in pairs or groups can work out different dialogues similar to the model provided, write them down and then act them out at the front of the classroom. (In the case of Doug and Dinsdale, the dialogue should perhaps be a police interrogation and confession).

Exercise nine
(C)

(Further oral practice of dates, familiarization with information to be used in later exercises)

This exercise can also be exploited for further practice of negative statements in contradiction to wrong statements of fact.

Exercise ten
(D)

(Oral practice of 'Who' + past tense questions and their short answer)

The 'yes/no' question can also be practised here:

Student 1 Did Cabral discover Australia?
Student 2 No, he didn't.

Student 1 Who discovered it?
Student 2 Hartog did. Etc.

Exercise eleven
(D)

(Further practice of 'When' questions in the past tense)
After some practice, exercises 10 and 11 can be combined:

Student 1 Who discovered the Pacific Ocean?
Student 2 Balboa (did).
Student 1 When did he discover it?
Student 1 In 1513. Etc.

Exercise twelve
(C)

(Further practice of times; oral practice of the infinitive of purpose)
By the end of this exercise, students can be asked to produce a series of connected sentences:

Student 1 Susan Brown went to the Centre to see the Sales Manager. She arrived there at ten to two and left at a quarter past three.

Exercise thirteen
(D)

(Further practice of questions in the past tense and the infinitive of purpose)
This exercise can also be used to draw the distinction between 'Who interviewed the director?' and 'Who did Marion Laker interview?'. This can be done with Marion Laker, Susan Brown, Inspector Blake and Elaine Smith.

Exercise fourteen
(E)

(Further writing practice of questions in the past tense)
The anticipated completions are:
a   When did Hartog discover
b   What time did Marion Laker
c   Columbus discover
d   Who discovered
e   Why did Marion Laker go to
f   When did Cabral discover
g   Why did Susan Brown go to

Exercise fifteen
(E)

(Further writing practice of questions in the past tense)
The anticipated completions are:
a   When did   e   What time did
b   Why did   f   Did
c   Who; did
d   Did; he did not

Exercise sixteen
(F)

(Further oral practice of the past tense)
Students can write variations of this dialogue in pairs and act them out at the front of the classroom.

Exercise seventeen

(Further oral practice: conversation)
This activity provides an opportunity for students to practise the past tense in contrast with the present simple. This can also be done in changing pairs (cf. Unit Eight, interaction sequence).

Reading comprehension (T) (G)

The answers are:

A 1 a   3 b   5 c
  2 c   4 b   6 c

B 1 T   3 T   5 F   7 T
  2 F   4 F   6 T   8 T

Interaction sequence (T) (H)

(Introduction and practice of some ways of expressing agreement and disagreement)
This can be seen as a continuation of the interaction sequence practised at the end of Unit Eight. The new adjectives will need some exemplification and practice, and students will perhaps ask for other words as the exchange of opinions continues. They should be asked to give opinions of well known books, films, television programmes, etc, as well as school subjects.

Unit ten

In this unit one way of referring to future time is
introduced and practised: 'is/am/are going to'. This type
of future reference is often called 'the future of
intention'. In fact, in this unit 'going to' is used in
connection both with intentions and impending events
which are the direct consequence of the present situation.
Other ways of referring to the future, notably by use of
the model auxiliary 'will' and by use of the present
progressive, are dealt with in later books.

The unit also contains some cumulative practice of the
present progressive and past tenses in contrast to 'going
to'.

PRONUNCIATION MODELS

It's going to rain. /its ˈgouiŋ tə ˋrein/

The boys are going to fall into the water. /ðə ˈboiz ə ˈgouiŋ
tə ˈfɔ:l intə ðə ˋwɔ:tə/

Where are they going to be on Friday? /ˈweər ə ðei ˈgouiŋ tə
ˈbiː ɔn ˋfraidei/

What are they going to do in London? /ˈwɔt ə ðəi ˈgouiŋ tə
ˈduː in ˋlʌndən/

Is she going to take him to the cinema? /iz ʃi ˈgouiŋ tə
ˈteik him tə ðə ˌsinəmɑː/

Exercise one
(C)

(Introduction and oral practice of 'is going to' and 'are
going to' in affirmative sentences)

Before beginning this exercise students should look
carefully at the pictures and work out by themselves
which verb from the box belongs with each picture.
(1 shave, 2 cut, 3 take, 4 fall, 5 rain, 6 be late for). Some
teachers may wish to convey the idea of futurity in the
classroom before beginning the exercise: this can be done
by demonstration, for example by preparing for an action,
and saying 'I'm going to . . . . . '.

Exercise two
(D)

(Oral practice of 'What's going to happen . . . . . ?', the use
of 'going to' in affirmative sentences and the present or
present progressive)

This exercise in four phases brings out clearly the

dependence of this sort of future reference on the present situation. The exercise allows for the introduction and practice of questions of the type: 'Is/are . . . . . going to . . . . . ?' and their answers.

Exercise three (E)

(Writing practice of 'is/are going to' in affirmative sentences, and questions)
The anticipated completions are:
a are going to fall into
b is going to rain
c is going to; are going to be late for the concert
d he is going to shave
e are going to cut the cake
f is Sally buying; is going to take

Exercise four ⓣ (A)

(Aural comprehension practice; familiarization with information to be used in oral practice)
Students should look carefully at the map and the accompanying 'brochure' of information, and understand clearly how they connect with each other before beginning this exercise.
The suggested sentences are:
1 They're going to stay at the Charles Hotel. (Monday and Tuesday)
2 They're going to take a boat trip on the canals. (Thursday)
3 They're going to fly to Spain. (Tomorrow)
4 They're going to travel to Brussels by train. (Wednesday)
5 They're going to visit London. (Friday and Saturday)
6 They're going to see a bullfight. (Tomorrow)
7 They're going to make a trip to Versailles and eat at an exclusive restaurant. (Monday and Tuesday)
8 They're going to see a play at the National Theatre and go shopping in the West End. (Friday and Saturday)
Note In this case students need write only the numbers of the sentences beside the appropriate days of the week.

Exercise five (C)

(Further practice of 'are going to' in affirmative and negative sentences)
The negative can be naturally introduced by mentioning some of the sights they are not going to see and things they are not going to do, or means of transport they are not going to use and countries and cities they are not going to visit:

109

<table>
<tr><td>Student 1</td><td>In London they are going to watch the changing of the guard but they aren't going to visit Westminster Abbey.</td></tr>
<tr><td>Student 2</td><td>They aren't going to visit Barcelona or Seville. Etc.</td></tr>
</table>

Exercise six ⓉⒹ   (Oral practice of 'going to' in various questions)

This exercise may be made more communicative by asking students to close their books. Questions can be asked in a coherent sequence:

<table>
<tr><td>Student 1</td><td>Where are they going to be on Wednesday?</td></tr>
<tr><td>Student 2</td><td>In Brussels.</td></tr>
<tr><td>Student 1</td><td>How are they going to travel there?</td></tr>
<tr><td>Student 2</td><td>By train.</td></tr>
<tr><td>Student 1</td><td>Where are they going to stay?</td></tr>
<tr><td>Student 2</td><td>At the Rex Hotel.</td></tr>
<tr><td>Student 1</td><td>What are they going to do in Brussels? Etc.</td></tr>
</table>

Exercise seven Ⓣ(F)   (Oral practice of 'yes/no' and other questions with 'going to')

This dialogue can be extended by using other questions students will already have practised.

Exercise eight (E)   (Further writing practice of 'going to')

The anticipated completions are:

a   are going to stay at the Rex
b   are going to travel
c   Are they going to stay (at the Charles Hotel) (for two days)
d   are they going to do; are going to visit
e   are they going to stay
f   Are they going to see; they are going to eat
g   are they going to be in Brussels (travel to Brussels)

Exercise nine   (Further oral practice of 'going to': conversation)

If a holiday is close it would be useful to ask students to list some details of their intentions: where they are going, where they are going to stay, how they are going to travel, what they are going to do, etc. The same can be done in a slightly more limited way with an approaching weekend. Students can then hold a short conversation in pairs, changing partners from time to time.

Exercise ten   (Oral and writing practice of 'I am going to')

Students can spend five minutes writing down resolutions for the future in pencil or on a separate piece of paper so that the teacher can check them. Students will almost certainly want some new vocabulary during this period. The teacher can then ask selected students to talk about their resolutions. Other students may occasionally wish to ask 'Why?', etc.

Exercise eleven
(C)

(Further oral practice of 'is going to')
   Negative statements are possible as alternatives in all cases with the exception of running and reading.

Exercise twelve

(Further writing practice: composition)
   Students should combine sentences with 'and' and 'but' or link them with pronouns.

Exercise thirteen
(F)

(Further oral practice)
   This dialogue provides an example of the natural use of 'going to' side by side with the present simple and other expressions.

Note 'going to go' is generally avoided. Students should notice that 'Where are you going?' is an example of the present progressive.

Exercise fourteen ⓣ
(D)

(Cumulative oral practice of the present progressive, past tense and 'going to')
   Students will need to look carefully at the pictures and understand how they relate to each other from left to right before beginning this activity. After mixed questions and answers, which can include 'yes/no' questions in the present, past or with 'going to', students can begin the six-phase exercise shown on the example.

Exercise fifteen
(E)

(Cumulative writing practice)
   The anticipated completions are:
a   bought a ticket to Rio
b   is studying/reading her history book
c   is going to paint the walls
d   is going to have dinner with her
e   took a book out of the library
f   is packing his suitcase

Note There is intentional variation in the kind of time adverbial used to refer to the future in the third column of pictures.

Reading
comprehension ⓣ
(C)

The answers are
A a T   c F   e T   g T
    b F   d T   f F   h T

B	1	F	3	F	5	T	7	F
	2	T	4	F	6	T	8	T

Interaction
sequence ⓣ
(H)

(Introduction and oral practice of some more ways of expressing agreement and disagreement)

This interaction sequence provides a follow on from the interaction sequence in the last unit. Students may be asked to fill out the 'questionnaire' for homework, before practising the sequence.

Third review and complementation unit

The following is a brief key to the exercises:

(Oral practice of questions in the past tense; practice of the distinction between 'Who' + past and 'What' + did)
Students may extend the list of inventions by personal research. The exercise can end with practice in four phases:
Student 1 Who invented the radio?
Student 2 Marconi (did).
Student 1 When did he invent it?
Student 2 In 1895. Etc.

Exercise two

The anticipated completions are:
1 invented the radio
2 did Bell invent the telephone
3 did Nobel
4 invent the printing press; he did
5 did he (Gutenberg) invent it (the printing press)
6 invented television; did
7 invent; invented the microscope
8 Marconi invent

Exercise three

(Practice of the present progressive, present simple and past)

1 went	5 gave	9 had
2 met	6 reads	10 is beginning
3 is writing	7 came	
4 costs	8 is running	

Exercise four

(Practice of mixed tenses)
are you doing; am reading; gave; bought; go; am cleaning; cut; is playing; does; plays

Exercise five

(Practice of word order)
1 Where did you go last night?
2 Was John at the party?
3 Who invented the radio?
4 Where did the Greens go for their last summer holidays?

5 How many books do you read every year?
6 I lent some money to my uncle.
7 (Please) put the cups on the shelf (please).
8 What time did the train arrive?

Exercise six

(Practice of prepositions)
On _____ at _____ at _____ of; at _____ in; into _____ through _____ on; up _____ to; on _____ in _____ in; of; after; over _____ across _____ to _____ on; at

Exercise seven

(Practice of questions in the past tense)
1 What happened
2 When was
3 What time did
4 Where were
5 Why did Mr Fielding
6 much did
7 What were the
8 Where were they
   (the paintings)
9 How many did the burglars
10 Who telephoned

Exercise eight

(Vocabulary)

spend	**government**	**horseback**
sell	taxes	underground
save	civil service	train
lend	defense	plane
buy		ship
eccentric	**remember**	**actor**
aggressive	recognise	painter
talented	think	waitress
amusing	know	dancer
		lecturer

Cumulative review exercises

This unit provides practice of several items dealt with in Book Two which teachers may feel students need extra practice in.

Exercise one

(Practice of past tense forms)

1 built	5 lent	9 slept
2 hit	6 sold	10 put
3 cut	7 understood	
4 heard	8 wore	

Exercise two

(Practice of past tense forms)

woke; felt _____ ate _____ drank; left _____ went; took; arrived; bought; cost

Exercise three

(Practice of word order)
1 What did you do last Saturday?
2 Who did you see at the party?
3 Who went with you to the party?
4 What is John going to do next Sunday?
5 Do you often go to France?
6 Where were the Browns?
7 Was Napoleon a tall man?
8 How much did they spend on education?
9 You do not often visit us.
10 How are they going to travel to Paris?

Exercise four

(Further practice of 'Why . . . . . ?', the infinitive of purpose and 'because')
'Get' can be used in the first two cases 'get some aspirins' and 'get a book') but 'have' should be used in the other two ('have a hamburger' and 'have a swim').

Exercise five

(Practice of prepositions; X = nothing)
X _____ through _____ to _____ with _____ X _____ from;
of _____ in _____ X _____ at; After _____ X _____ in _____
of _____ between; in; with _____ of; on _____ to; into
_____ through _____ to; X _____ after

Exercise six

(Distinction between regular and irregular past tense forms)

wanted	cut	spent
stayed	put	sent
happened	hit	learnt
liked	cost	built
imported	read*	got
lived		fell
needed		met
talked		found
deposited		
wanted		

*Note The spelling of the past tense form of 'read' is the same as the present tense although the pronunciation is different /red/.

Exercise seven

(Practice of mixed tenses)

1 made
2 is going to bring
3 ate
4 am going to write
5 pays
6 took
7 are buying
8 is going to leave
9 paints
10 is cutting

Cumulative lexis list for Pupils' Books 1 and 2

R = Review Unit
P = passive language

1.1 etc. = (Book one, Unit One etc.)
2.1 = (Book Two, Unit One, etc.)

A

a (1.1)
a lot (1.9)
ability (1.6)
Aborigine (1.10P)
about (1.8)
accent (1.7P)
according to (1.9P)
account (1. (n.) 10)
accurate (1.8P)
across (1.6P)
active (1.3)
activity (2.2)
actor (1.3)
actress (1.3)
address (1.(n)8)
adult (2.1P)
advance (2.8P)
advertisement (1.9P)
aeroplane (2.3)
affair (1.8P)
afraid (2.6P)
African (1.6)
after (2.2)
afternoon (1.7)
again (1.4)
age (1.(n)8)
aggressive (2.9P)
ago (2.4P)
agree (2.9)
agricultural (1.7P)
air (2.1P)
airline (2.3P)
airport (1.R3)

all (1.1)
all right (1.7)
almond (2.2)
almost (1.8P)
alone (1.5)
along (2.6)
already (2.10)
also (1.7P)
although (1.8P)
always (1.10)
amateur (2.3P)
amazing (2.7P)
amusing (2.7)
anaesthetic (1.4P)
anaesthetist (1.4P)
ancient (2.8P)
and (1.2)
Anglo-Saxon (1.7P)
animal (2.3)
annual (2.3)
another (1.5P)
answer (2.(n)3P)
antelope (1.8)
anthropologist (2.3P)
any (2.2)
apart (2.2P)
appendicitis (2.R3)
apple (1.1)
application form (1.6)
appointment (2.3)
April (1.4)
architecture (1.8)
are (1.1)
area (1.3P)

arm (1.R1)
armchair (2.R1)
around (1.9P)
arrival (1.7P)
arrive (1.7)
arrow (1.6P)
art (2.8)
artery (1.4P)
artesian well (1.10P)
article (2.R1)
as (1.4P)
as usual (2.1P)
as well as (2.3P)
aspirin (2.2)
assignment (2.3)
assist (1.5)
assistant (1.2)
astonished (2.9P)
at (1.2P)
at least (2.7P)
at the moment (2.3)
attack (2.6P)
attend (1.10)
attractive (2.7)
August (1.4)
aunt (2.5)
authenticity (2.1P)
author (2.1P)
authority (2.9P)
autograph (1.3)
available (2.2)
avenue (1.3P)
average (1.9)
away (1.8P)

117

axe (2.R3)

B

baboon (1.8)
baby (2.7)
back (2.3P)
bacon (1.8)
bad (2.2P)
bag (1.4)
baker (2.7P)
baking powder (2.2)
ballroom (2.1)
banana (1.3)
bank (1.R2)
banker (2.7)
bar (2.1P)
barber shop (2.1P)
bat (2.6P)
bathroom (1.5)
bathyscope (2.10P)
be based (2.6P)
be born (2.9P)
beach (2.8)
bear (1.10P)
beard (1.3)
beat (2.9P)
beautiful (2.7)
because (1.7)
become (2.8)
bed (1.4)
bedroom (1.5)
bee (2.9P)
beer (1.8)
before (2.2)
begin (1.7)
being (2.10P)
below (2.8P)
berry (2.4P)
beside (2.6)
besides (2.10P)
best (1.9P)
between (2.6)
bicycle (1.6)
big (1.3)
billion (1.1)
bird (2.6P)
birth (1.3)

birthday (2.5)
biscuit (1.9)
bite (2.6P)
black (1.3)
blackboard (1.4)
blender (1.10)
block (2.3)
blood (1.4P)
blouse (1.4)
blue (1.3)
board meeting (2.4)
boardroom (2.7)
boat (1.8P)
body (1.4P)
bone (2.8P)
book (1.1)
bookshop (2.2P)
book stall (2.1)
border (2.5P)
boring (2.8)
boss (2.5)
botanist (2.3P)
both (1.8P)
bottle (1.(adj.)2)
bowl (1.R3)
box (2.1)
boxer (2.9P)
boy (1.3)
branch (2.10)
brave (2.7)
bread (1.9)
breadcrumbs (2.2)
break (2.7)
breakfast (1.5)
breakfast room (1.9)
bridge (2.3)
bright (1.9P)
bring (2.10P)
British (1.5)
broken (2.1)
bronze (2.8P)
brooch (2.8P)
brother (1.4)
brother-in-law (2.5)
brown (1.3)
budget (2.4)
build (2.3)

building (1.7)
bullfight (2.10)
burglar (2.9)
bus (1.7)
bus station (1.1)
Bushman (1.6P)
busy (2.1)
but (1.4)
butter (2.2)
butterfly (2.9P)
buy (1.5)
by (1.7)

C

cafetaria (2.1)
cake (2.2)
calculator (1.R3)
calendar (1.1)
call (1.(v.)6P)
camera (1.5)
cameraman (1.5)
camping (2.4P)
campsite (1.6P)
can (1.(v.)3)
canal (2.3)
candidate (2.4)
cape (1.6P)
capital (1.5P)
car (1.3)
card (1.9)
cardiologist (1.2P)
careful (2.1P)
carefully (1.4P)
carpenter (1.4)
carrot (1.3)
carry (1.6P)
carve (1.8P)
cashier (1.10)
casino (2.1P)
catch (1.(v.)8P)
cathedral (2.1)
cause (2.(v.)6P)
cave (1.6P)
Celtic (1.7P)
centigrade (1.5P)
centimetre (1.3)

central (2.1)
centre (1.10P)
century (2.10)
cereal (2.1)
ceremonial (1.7P)
ceremony (1.8P)
chair (1.1)
chairman (2.5)
champion (2.9P)
championship (2.7)
change (1.(v.)10)
channel (2.2P)
characteristic (1.(n.adj.)7P)
charming (2.8)
cheap (1.3)
check (2.3P)
cheetah (1.8)
chemist (2.2)
chess (1.6)
cheque (1.10)
chicken (2.2)
chimpanzee (1.8)
chip (2.3P)
chocolate (2.1)
choir (2.5)
church (1.1)
cigar (2.1)
cigarette (1.3)
cinema (1.1)
circuit (2.3P)
city (1.R1)
civil engineer (2.3)
civil service (2.8)
class (1.R2)
classical (2.4)
clean (1.(v.)5)
cleaner (1.10)
clever (2.7)
climate (1.10P)
clock (1.1)
close (1.4)
clothes (2.4)
clothing (1.8P)
cloud (2.10)
coal (1.10P)
coat (1.4)

coffee (1.1)
coffee pot (1.1)
coin (2.8P)
cold (1.4)
collect (2.5)
college (2.1)
colony (2.4P)
colour (1.3)
come in (1.6)
comfortable (1.3)
committee (2.5)
common (1.8P)
commune (1.8P)
community (1.8P)
company (1.9)
compare (2.1P)
complete (2.2P)
complex (1.6P)
composer (2.7)
computer (1.3)
computerized (1.3)
concert (1.7)
condition (1.5P)
connect (1.4P)
conscientious objector (2.9P)
consent (1.(v.)8P)
consume (1.9)
contact (1.6P)
contain (2.4P)
continent (1.10P)
continue (2.6)
contrast (2.4P)
control (1.(v.)8P)
convention room (2.1)
cool (1.(n.)7P)
cool (1.(adj.)4)
copper (1.10P)
corn (2.4P)
corner (1.10)
cornflakes (1.8)
cost (1.(v.)10)
costume (1.7P)
cottage (1.9)
counter (2.3P)
country (1.9)
countryside (2.4P)

cousin (2.5)
cover (2(v.)8P)
cow (2.6P)
craft (2.2P)
crater (2.9P)
creature (2.6P)
cross (2.(v.)1)
crowd (1.5P)
cultivate (2.8P)
culture (1.6P)
cup (1.1)
cupboard (1.1)
currency (1.10)
cushion (2.2P)
custom (2.4P)
customer (1.5)
cut (2.(v.)8P)
cutting ((2.(n.)2P)

D
dagger (2.8P)
dairy (1.10P)
dam (2.3)
dancer (2.7)
dangerous (2.6P)
dark (1.3)
daughter (2.5)
daytime (2.4)
dead (2.6P)
dear (1.2)
death (1.4P)
December (1.4)
decision (2.4)
deep (2.4P)
deer (1.8)
defence (2.8)
delicious (2.5P)
deliver (2.9)
dentist (1.3)
depart (2.6)
departure (1.7)
deposit (2.(n.)3)
deposit (1.(v.)10)
depth (2.10P)
desert (1.6P)
desk (1.1)
design (2.3)

designer (2.3)
destination (1.7)
destroy (2.7P)
develop (2.4P)
diagnosis (2.3P)
diagram (1.6)
dialect (1.6P)
diary (2.5P)
die (2.7P)
different (1.7P)
difficult (1.4P)
dining room (1.5)
dinner (1.R2)
direct (2.2P)
directly (2.2P)
director (1.5)
dirty (2.7P)
disagree (2.9)
discover (2.8)
discovery (2.8)
diseased (1.4P)
dismantle (1.6P)
distance (1.9P)
diver (2.10P)
diving-suit (2.10P)
do (1.(v.)5)
do (1.(aux.)5)
doctor (1.4)
documentary (2.3)
does (1.(aux.)1)
dog (1.8)
dollar (1.8)
door (1.4)
doorway (2.8P)
double (2.1)
double-decker (1.9P)
doughnut (1.9)
down (2.6)
downtown (1.3P)
drain (2.7P)
draw (1.6)
drawer (1.1)
dress (1.(n.)7P)
drink (1.(v.)8)
drink (1.(n.)9)
drive (1.6)
driving licence (1.6)

dry (1.4)
dull (2.10)
during (1.R3)
duty (1.10)
dynamite (2.R3)

E
each (1.2)
ear-ring (2.8P)
early (2.4)
earn (1.8)
earthquake (2.9P)
east (1.2)
easy (2.9)
eat (1.5)
eccentric (2.7)
economic (1.6P)
economist (2.7)
edible (2.4P)
edition (2.10P)
education (2.3P)
efficient (1.9P)
egg (1.8)
eight (1.1)
eighteen (1.1)
eighty (1.1)
electric saw (2.2)
electrical (2.3)
eleven (1.1)
employee (2.1)
empty (2.9)
energy (2.3P)
engaged (2.7)
engineer (1.4)
engineering (1.9)
English (1.5)
enjoy (2.6)
enjoyable (2.6P)
enormous (2.1P)
enthusiastic (2.3P)
equipment (2.3)
erupt (2.6P)
Eskimo (1.8P)
especially (1.8)
establish (2.6P)
estimate (1.8P)
evaporated milk (2.2)

evening (2.2)
every (1.9)
everybody (2.3P)
everything (1.8P)
evidence (2.8P)
exactly (1.6P)
examination (1.9P)
example (2.3P)
excavate (2.8P)
excavation (2.8P)
except (2.10)
exchange (2.8)
executive (2.5)
excited (2.2P)
exciting (1.3P)
exclusive (2.10)
excursion (2.10)
excuse (1.(v.)1)
exercise (1(n.)3)
expand (2.3)
expect (2.3P)
expedition (2.1P)
expensive (1.3)
experiment (2.10P)
expert (1.9P)
exploration (2.10P)
explorer (2.7)
export (2.(v.)3)
export (2.(n.)3)
extensive (1.9P)
extract (2.10P)
eye (1.3)

F
fabulous (2.9P)
face (1.4P)
facility (2.1)
factory (1.5)
fahrenheit (1.5P)
fair (1.3)
fall (2.(v.)3)
falls (2.5P)
family (1.4)
famous (2.7)
fantastic (2.1)
far (2.6)

fare (1.9P)
farm (1.8)
farmer (2.8)
fascinating (2.1P)
fast (1.3)
fat (2.7)
father (1.4)
fauna (1.10P)
feat (2.3P)
feature (2.8P)
February (1.4)
feel (2.2P)
fellow (2.10P)
ferry (2.6)
fertile (2.4P)
festival (1.7P)
few (2.R2)
fiancée (2.4P)
fifteen (1.1)
fifth (2.10)
fifty (1.1)
fight (2.8P)
figure (2.8P)
filling (2.2)
film (1.(n.)5)
find (1.(v.)5)
fine (1.6)
finish (1.(v.)7)
fire (2.7P)
fire extinguisher (2.9)
first (1.5)
fish (1.(n.)8)
fish (1.(v.)8P)
five (1.1)
flat (1.5P)
flight (1.R2)
float (2.(v.)2P)
floating (2.(adj.)1P)
flour (2.2)
flower (1.6P)
fly (1.(v.)6)
fly (2.(n.)7P)
following (2.6P)
food (1.8)
foot (1.3)
football (1.R1)
for (2.1)

for example (1.3P)
foreign (1.6)
forest (1.8)
fork (1.2)
form (1.(v.)7P)
forty (1.1)
found (1.(v.)3P)
four (1.1)
fourteen (1.1)
fourth (2.10)
French (1.5)
fresh (2.4P)
Friday (1.7)
friend (2.1)
friendly (2.4P)
frightening (2.10P)
from (1.3)
fruit (1.8)
fuel (1.9)
full (1.9P)
fun (2.9P)
fund (2.5)
furniture (2.3)
future (1.10P)

G
gallery (1.7)
gallon (1.9)
game (1.5P)
garage (2.3)
gate (2.6)
gather (1.6P)
gas (2.10P)
generally (1.5P)
geography (1.2P)
geologist (2.3)
German (1.6)
get (2.2P)
get married (2.4)
get up (1.8)
geyser (2.6P)
girl (1.3)
glass (1.2)
glasses (1.4)
glove (1.4P)
go (1.R2)
God (1.6P)

gold (1.10P)
golf (1.7)
good (1.4)
good afternoon (1.6)
goodbye (1.6)
good evening (1.6)
good morning (1.6)
good night (1.6)
government (2.8)
gown (1.7P)
graceful (2.7)
gram (2.2)
grandfather (1.10)
grandmother (1.10)
grave (2.(n.)6P)
green (1.3)
greengrocer (2.2P)
grey (1.3)
grizzly bear (2.6P)
ground (1.(adj.)5)
group (2.3)
grow (2.8P)
guide (2.6P)
guitar (1.6)
gymnasium (2.1P)

H
hair (1.3)
hairdresser (2.1P)
half (2.2)
ham (1.8)
hamburger (2.5P)
hammer (2.2)
hand (1.4)
handbag (2.5)
happen (2.10)
hard (1.4P)
harmless (2.6P)
has/have to (2.4)
hat (1.4)
have (1.3)
he (1.3)
headache (2.7)
headquarters (2.6P)
health (2.8)
hear (2.3)
heart (2.9)

heavy (2.3P)
height (1.3)
hello (1.R1)
help (1.(v.)5)
helpful (2.6P)
her (1.(poss.adj.)3)
her (1.(pro.)5)
here (1.1)
hero (1.6P)
hey! (1.8)
hi! (1.6)
high (1.2P)
hill (2.6)
him (1.5)
himself (2.9P)
his (1.4)
history (2.8)
hit (2.9)
hobby (2.5)
hold (2.10)
hole (2.7)
holiday (2.1)
home (1.5)
homework (1.5)
hope (2.(v.)3P)
horse (1.R3)
hospital (1.1)
hot (1.4)
hotel (1.1)
hour (2.2P)
house (1.2P)
household (2.3)
housewife (1.4)
housing (1.5P)
hovercraft (2.2P)
how (1.3)
however (1.10P)
human (2.9)
hundred (1.1)
hunger (1.9)
hungry (1.9)
hunt (1.(v.)8P)
husband (1.4)
hut (2.9)
hydro-carbon (2.10P)
hydrophobia (2.6P)

I
I (1.3P)
Iberian (1.7P)
ice (1.8P)
idea (2.8)
identify (2.3P)
ill (2.2P)
illness (2.2P)
immediately (2.4)
immigrant (2.4P)
import (2.3)
important (2.8)
impossible (2.8)
improve (2.3)
in (1.1)
in fact (1.8P)
in front of (1.2P)
inch (1.3)
include (2.6P)
increase (1.(v.)5P)
independent (2.8P)
indian (2.6P)
industrial (2.5P)
industry (2.8)
information (2.1P)
informed (2.10)
inhabitant (2.7P)
injection (2.R3)
insect (2.6P)
inside (1.9P)
inspect (2.9)
instrument (1.4P)
insulating tape (2.2)
intend (2.4P)
interest (2.(n.)1P)
interesting (1.10P)
interior (2.10P)
interview (2.(v.)3)
into (2.2P)
introduce (2.4P)
invent (2.R3)
invention (2.R3)
inventory (2.R1)
invitation (2.3P)
invite (2.3P)
iron ore (1.10P)
irrelevant (2.9)

is (1.1)
island (1.3P)
issue (2.5)
it (1.1)
Italian (1.5)
item (2.3P)
its (1.3P)
ivory (1.8P)

J
jail (2.7)
January (1.4)
jar (2.2)
jazz (2.4P)
jet (2.1P)
jewellery (2.8P)
job (2.4)
join (2.3P)
jug (2.8P)
juice (1.1)
July (1.4)
June (1.4)
jungle (2.4P)
just (a minute!) (1.5)
journey (1.9P)

K
kangaroo (1.10P)
keep (2.3P)
kill (1.6P)
kilo (1.8)
kind (2.4P)
kitchen (1.5)
knife (1.2)
knit (1.6)
knock (2.1)
know (1.8P)

L
label (2.3P)
ladder (2.2)
lady (2.1P)
lake (1.3P)
land (1.7P)
landscape (2.4P)
language (1.6)
large (1.7)

last (2.(v.)7P)
last (2.(adj.)2P)
late (2.3P)
later (1.6)
latitude (1.8P)
law (1.7)
lawyer (1.8)
leader (2.3P)
leaf (1.8)
leave (1.R2)
lecturer (1.3)
left (1.R1)
leg (1.8P)
legend (2.6P)
lemon (2.2)
lend (1.4)
let's (1.R2)
letter (1.5)
lettuce (1.3)
level crossing (2.1)
library (2.1P)
licence (2.9P)
lie (2.2P)
life (1.4P)
lift (2.(v.)2P)
light (2.3)
lighter (1.1)
like (1.(adv.)4)
like (2.(v.)4)
linguist (2.10P)
listen (1.5)
literature (2.8)
little (1.6)
live (1.8)
living room (1.5)
loaf (2.8)
loan (1.10)
local (1.6P)
locate (2.10P)
loincloth (1.6P)
long (1.5)
look (1.(v.)3)
look after (2.1P)
look forward (2.2P)
look out (2.1)
loud (2.3)
Ltd. (2.1P)

luck (2.4P)
luckily (2.7P)
lucky (2.2P)
luggage (2.5P)
lunch (1.(n.)R3)
lunch (2.(v.)1)
lung (1.4P)
luxury (1.9P)

M
machine (1.4P)
madam (1.1)
magazine (2.5)
magnificent (2.7P)
maiden (2.5)
main (1.4P)
major (2.4P)
majority (1.10P)
make (1.5)
make-up (1.5)
mammal (2.6P)
man (1.3)
manage (2.3)
manager (1.10)
manganese (2.10P)
many (1.3P)
map (1.R1)
March (1.4)
market (2.1)
marriage (1.8P)
marsupial (1.10P)
mask (1.4P)
match (2.4)
maths (1.9)
matter (1.4P)
May (1.4)
may (1.8P)
mayonnaise (2.2)
me (1.1)
meal (1.R3)
mean (1.10)
meat (1.8)
mechanical (2.3)
medal (2.9P)
medicine (2.3P)
medium (2.9P)
meet (2.4)

meeting (2.7)
member (2.5)
mend (2.(v.)7)
metre (1.2P)
Mexican (1.5)
microphone (2.3)
microscope (2.R3)
middle (1.3P)
midnight (1.6)
midwest (1.2)
mile (1.5P)
milk (2.2)
million (1.1)
mine (1.R2)
mineral (1.10P)
mining (2.10P)
minister (2.7)
minute (1.6)
mist (2.5P)
mobile home (1.8)
model (1.3)
modern (1.4)
money (1.R3)
month (1.3P)
moon (2.9)
morning (2.1)
mosaic (2.8P)
mosquito (2.6P)
most (1.6P)
motel (1.1)
mother (1.4)
motorway (2.5P)
move (1.(v.)5P)
much (1.4)
muscular (2.7)
museum (1.7)
mushroom (2.2)
music (1.4)
musician (1.7P)
must (2.10P)
mustard (2.2)
mutual (1.8P)
my (1.R1)

N
nail (2.2)
name (1.3)

narrow (2.2P)
national (1.9P)
native (2.3P)
near (1.1)
nearby (1.9P)
nearly (1.4P)
necessary (1.4P)
necklace (2.8P)
need (2.(v.)1)
neighbouring (2.4P)
nephew (2.5)
newsagent (2.2)
newspaper (1.8)
next (1.6)
niece (2.5)
night club (1.10)
night-watchman (2.4)
nine (1.1)
nineteen (1.1)
ninety (1.1)
no (1.1)
nomadic (1.6P)
noon (1.6)
north (1.2)
not (1.1)
note (2.1P)
notebook (2.2)
nothing (2.4)
novel (2.4)
November (1.4)
now (1.5P)
number (1.5P)
nurse (1.4P)
nut (2.1)

O

object (1.8P)
observe (1.5)
occasion (1.7P)
occupation (1.3)
ocean (2.2P)
o'clock (1.6)
October (1.4)
of (1.3)
of course (1.3)
off (2.2P)
offer (2.4P)

office (2.3)
oil (2.3)
OK (1.6)
old (1.2P)
olive oil (2.2)
omelette (2.2)
on (1.1)
once (1.9)
one (1.1)
onion (1.3)
only (2.1)
open (1.(v.)4)
open (1.(adj.)8)
opera singer (1.3)
operate (1.4P)
operation (1.4P)
opinion (2.7P)
opposite (1.2P)
orange (1.1)
ordinary (1.9P)
ore (2.10P)
organiser (2.5)
origin (1.7P)
other (1.6)
our (1.4)
ours (1.R2)
outside (2.4)
over (2.1)
overland (2.4P)
own (1.7P)

P

pack (2.10)
packet (2.1)
paint (2.(n.)1)
paint (2.(v.)3)
painter (2.7)
painting (1.6P)
pair (1.6P)
paradise (2.4P)
parents (2.R1)
park (2.1)
parking (2.3)
part (2.3)
particularly (1.10P)
party (1.10)
pass (2.(v.)5P)

passenger (2.1P)
passport (1.7P)
past (1.6)
patient (1.4P)
pay for (2.4)
pea (1.3)
peace (2.1P)
peel (2.2)
pen (1.1)
pencil (1.3)
people (1.4P)
pepper (2.2)
per (1.6)
perfect (2.2P)
perform (1.4P)
period (2.8)
person (1.6)
personnel manager (1.5)
petrol station (2.8)
phone (1.10)
photograph (2.2P)
photographer (2.3)
piano (1.6)
picnic (1.5P)
picture (1.3)
pie (1.9)
piece (2.8P)
pig (2.8P)
pillow (2.5)
pipe (1.1)
place (1.3)
plague (2.7P)
plain (2.4P)
plan (1.6)
plane (1.6)
plant (2.(v.)3)
plant (2.(n.)3P)
plantation (2.6P)
plastic (1.4P)
plate (1.2)
platform (2.10P)
play (2.(n.)4)
play (1.(v.)5)
please (1.1)
pleasure (1.4)
plough (2.8P)
pneumonia (2.4)

pocket calculator (2.3P)
poet (1.7P)
poetry (1.7P)
poisoned (1.6P)
Polar (1.8P)
policeman (2.4)
polish (2.1P)
politics (2.8)
popular (2.6P)
population (1.5P)
port (2.2P)
portable (2.4P)
Portuguese (1.6)
post (2.8P)
postcard (1.1)
post office (1.1)
potato (2.2)
pottery (2.8P)
pound (1.2)
powerful (1.8P)
prairie (2.4P)
predict (1.5P)
prefer (1.10)
preparations (2.2P)
prepare (2.4)
president (1.5)
press (2.7)
pretty (2.8)
prevent (1.9P)
previously (2.10P)
price (2.8)
print (2.(v.)3P)
printing press (2.8)
prison (2.1)
probably (1.8P)
problem (1.5P)
product (2.3)
production (1.5)
professional (2.9P)
programme (2.1)
programmer (2.1)
progress (2.3)
project (2.3)
prominent (2.3P)
property (1.6P)
prospect (2.(v.)3)
provide (1.4P)

public (1.9P)
publication (2.1P)
publicity (2.2P)
publish (2.10P)
pudding (2.2)
pull (1.(v.)8P)
puma (1.8)
pump (1.(v.)4P)
purchase (1.5)
put (1.2)
put on (1.5)

Q
quarter (1.6)
question (2.3)
questionnaire (2.4)
quickly (1.6)
quiet (2.(adj.)7P)
quietly (2.3)
quite (2.6P)

R
rabies (2.6P)
racing driver (2.3)
racial (1.7P)
radio (2.3P)
railway (2.10P)
rain (1.10P)
rainfall (1.4)
raise (1.8)
rapidly (1.5P)
rat (2.7P)
razor (2.10)
reach (2.9)
read (1.5)
ready (2.2P)
real (2.1P)
really? (1.3)
receipt (2.3P)
receive (1.10)
recent (2.1P)
receptionist (1.8)
recognise (2.8)
record (2.(n.)5)
recording (2.7P)
red (1.3)
reduce (1.9P)

reformation (2.8)
refrigerator (1.10)
refuse (2.9P)
regain (2.9P)
region (1.6P)
relative (2.10P)
relevant (2.9)
religion (2.8)
remains (2.8P)
remarkable (2.8P)
remember (2.8)
rent (1.(n.)8)
repair (2.4P)
replace (1.4P)
reply (2.1)
report (1.(n.)5)
reporter (2.3P)
research (2.4)
reservation (2.7P)
reserves (1.10P)
resort (2.7P)
resource (2.10P)
respond (1.5)
rest (2.(n.)7P)
rest (2.(v.)9P)
restaurant (1.1)
result (2.8P)
return (2.6)
rice (2.2)
rich (1.10P)
ride (1.6)
right (1.(adj.)1)
rise (2.3)
river (1.3P)
road (2.1)
robbery (2.8)
rock (1.6P)
rocky (1.8)
roof (1.9P)
room (2.1)
root (1.6P)
rough (2.2P)
round (1.(adv.)4P)
route (2.6)
rubber (2.2P)
ruined (2.(adj.)4P)
ruins (2.1)

run (2.1P)
rush-hour (1.9P)

S

sail (1.(v.)8P)
salary (1.9)
sale (2.3)
salesman (1.3)
sales manager (1.4P)
salt (2.2)
same (1.4P)
sample (2.4P)
sandwich (1.1)
Saturday (1.7)
saucer (1.2)
save (2.3P)
say (1.4)
scenery (2.6)
school (1.R1)
schoolboy (1.R3)
schoolgirl (1.4)
science (2.8P)
scientist (2.3P)
Scottish (1.7P)
scratch (2.8P)
screw (2.2)
script (1.5)
sculpture (2.8)
sea (2.1P)
seal (2.3)
seaside (2.7P)
secondary (1.2P)
secondly (2.6P)
secretary (1.3)
sect (2.9P)
security officer (2.9)
see (1.3P)
sell (2.3)
send (2.2P)
sentence (2.(v.)9P)
September (1.4)
serene (2.7P)
serious (1.5P)
serve (2.1P)
settlement (2.7P)
seven (1.1)
seventeen (1.1)

seventh (2.10)
seventy (1.1)
several (1.7P)
shall (2.(aux.)5)
share (1(v.)8P)
shark (2.9P)
shave (2.10)
she (1.3)
sheep (1.8)
shelf (1.1)
ship (2.1P)
shirt (1.4)
shoe (1.4)
shoemender (2.4P)
shop (2.1)
shopping centre (2.1)
shore (2.5P)
short (1.3)
shorthand (1.6)
shoulder (1.6P)
show (1.9P)
shower (2.R1)
sickle (2.8P)
side (1.4P)
sight (2.5P)
silicon (2.3P)
silver (1.10P)
similar (1.8P)
simple (2.8P)
since (2.10P)
sing (1.5)
singer (1.3)
single (2.7)
sir (1.1)
sister (1.4)
sit down (1.R3)
site (2.8P)
six (1.1)
sixteen (1.1)
sixth (2.10)
sixty (1.1)
ski (1.6)
skiing (2.9)
skilled (2.8P)
skin (1.6P)
skirt (2.5)
skyscraper (2.5P)

slave (2.8P)
sled (1.8P)
sleep (2.3)
sleeping bag (2.4P)
slim (1.3)
slippery (2.1)
slow (1.3)
slowly (1.5P)
small (1.3)
smell (2.7P)
smog (2.1P)
smoke (1.(v.)8)
smoke (2.(n.)9P)
snow (1.8P)
so (2.R1)
social (2.3)
society (1.8P)
sociology (2.1P)
socket (2.2)
soft drink (1.9)
solo (1.7P)
some (2.2)
someone (2.2P)
sometimes (2.10)
son (2.5)
song (1.5)
soon (2.3P)
sorry (1.5)
soup (2.2)
source (1.10P)
south (1.2)
space (2.3)
spare (2.2)
Spanish (1.6)
speak (1.5)
spear (2.8P)
special (1.4P)
speech (2.7)
spend (1.8)
spoon (1.2)
spoonful (2.2)
sponsor (2.10P)
sports club (2.1)
spread (2.7P)
spring (2.6)
square (1.7)
squash (2.3)

stadium (2.1)
staff (2.1P)
stairs (2.5P)
stamp (2.2P)
star (1.5)
start (2.7P)
state (2.4P)
stay (2.4)
steamer (2.10P)
sterilize (1.4P)
stimulating (2.9)
sting (2.9P)
stock (2.R1)
stone (1.7)
stop (1.7)
stove (1.10)
straight (2.6)
strange (1.10P)
street (1.R1)
stretch (2.(v.)4P)
stretcher (2.R3)
strong (2.7)
student (1.3)
studio (2.3)
study (1.(v.)5)
study (2.(n.)1P)
submarine (2.10P)
suburb (1.8)
suburban (1.9P)
suddenly (2.7P)
sugar (2.2)
suggest (2.7)
suitable (1.5P)
suitcase (1.8)
suite (2.1)
summarise (2.10P)
summer (1.5P)
sunbathe (2.6P)
Sunday (1.7)
sunny (2.5P)
sunset (2.1P)
supermarket (2.2)
surface (2.9P)
surgeon (1.4P)
surgery (1.4P)
surgical (1.4P)
surprisingly (2.5P)

swamp (2.9P)
sweater (2.6)
sweep (1.10)
sweet (2.1)
swim (1.6)
swimming-pool (1.9)
switch (2.2)
symbol (1.9P)
system (1.8P)

T
table (1.2)
take (1.6)
take off (2.3P)
tail (2.R2)
talented (2.7)
talk (1.5)
tall (1.3)
tape (2.1P)
tape recorder (2.4P)
tax (2.10)
taxi driver (1.8)
tea (1.9)
teach (1.7)
teacher (2.7)
team (2.7)
teaspoonful (2.2)
technology (2.3P)
tedious (2.9)
telephone (1.1)
television (1.10)
tell (2.1)
temperate (1.10P)
temperature (1.4)
temple (2.8P)
ten (1.1)
ten-pin bowling (2.7)
tennis (2.3)
tennis-court (2.R1)
tent (2.4P)
terrible (2.5P)
that (1.1)
thatched (1.6P)
the (1.1)
theatre (1.9)
their (1.4)
theirs (1.R2)

them (1.5)
then (1.10)
there (1.(adv.)R2)
there is/are (2.1)
these (1.R1)
they (1.2)
thief (2.9)
thing (2.8P)
think (2.3P)
third (2.6)
thirst (1.9)
thirsty (1.9)
thirteen (1.1)
thirty (1.1)
this (1.1)
those (1.R1)
thousand (1.1)
three (1.1)
through (2.6)
throw (2.7P)
Thursday (1.7)
ticket (1.4)
time (1.6)
tin (2.1)
tired (1.4P)
title (2.9P)
toaster (1.10)
tobacconist (2.2)
today (1.R2)
tomorrow (1.7)
tonight (1.7)
too (1.2)
tool (2.8P)
toolbox (2.2)
toothache (2.7)
top (1.(adj.)2)
total (1.5P)
tour (2.6)
tower (1.7)
town (1.R1)
Town Hall (2.6P)
tractor (2.3)
tradition (1.7P)
traditional (1.6P)
traffic (1.5P)
train (2.1)
train (2.(v.)8)

trainer (2.9P)
transmit (2.6P)
transplant (2.9)
transport (1.9P)
trap (1.(v.)8P)
travel (1.7)
travel agency (2.1)
treasurer (2.5)
treatment (2.3P)
tree (1.9)
tremendous (2.5P)
tribe (1.6P)
trip (1.4)
triumph (2.3P)
tropical (2.4P)
trousers (1.4)
truck (2.3)
true (2.1P)
tube (1.9P)
Tuesday (1.7)
tunnel (2.R2)
turbine (2.2P)
turf (1.8P)
turn off (2.3)
TV (1.9)
twelve (1.1)
twenty (1.1)
twice (1.9)
twin (2.6)
two (1.1)
type (1.5)
typewriter (1.1)
typical (2.5P)
typing (1.6)
tyre (2.3)

U
umbrella (1.5)
unaverage (1.9)
uncomfortable (1.3)
under (1.4)
underground (1.5)
understand (2.1P)
underwear (2.6)
unfortunately (2.7P)
unified (2.8P)
uniform (2.4)

union (2.4P)
unit (1.8P)
university (1.R2)
unknown (2.4P)
unpleasant (2.8)
unusual (1.10P)
up (2.6)
upside-down (2.6P)
uranium (1.10P)
us (1.R2)
use (1.(v.)7P)
use (2.(n.)3P)
usually (1.R2)

V
valley (2.6)
valuable (2.10P)
value (1.4P)
vampire (2.6P)
van (2.2)
vapour (2.5P)
various (1.6P)
vary (1.9P)
vehicle (1.9P)
vein (1.4P)
very (1.3)
victim (2.6P)
view (2.6)
visit (1.(v.)5)
visitor (2.6P)
vivid (1.6P)
volcano (2.6P)
volleyball (1.8)
voyage (2.1P)

W
wait (1.(v.)R2)
waitress (2.7)
wallaby (1.10P)
wander (1.6P)
want (2.1)
warm (1.4)
was/were (2.7)
wash (1.10)
washing machine (1.10)
watch (1.(n.)5)

watch (2.(v.)P)
water (1.9)
way (1.4P)
we (1.R1)
weapon (2.8)
wear (2.4)
weather (1.4)
Wednesday (1.7)
week (1.9)
weekend (1.8)
welcome (1(adj.)1)
well (1.(adv.)6)
Welsh (1.7P)
west (1.2)
wet (1.4)
what (1.1)
wheat (2.4P)
when (1.4P)
where? (1.1)
whether (2.4P)
which (1.(rel.pro.)10P)
while (2.6P)
white (1.3)
who (1.(inter.pro.)3)
who (2.(rel.pro.)2P)
whole (1.10P)
whose? (2.5)
why? (1.7)
wide (1.3P)
wife (1.4)
wild (1.6P)
will (1.(aux.)4)
win (2.8)
windmill (2.10)
window (1.4)
windy (2.4P)
wing-span (2.6P)
winner (2.7)
winter (1.5P)
wire (2.2)
with (1.3)
without (1.4P)
woman (1.3)
wonderful (2.6P)
wood (1.8P)
wooden (2.8P)
work (2.(v.)3)

work (1.(n.)7)
worker (2.8P)
world (1.8P)
worried (2.10P)
would (1.(aux.)9)
write (1.4)
writer (1.3)

Y

year (1.3)
yellow (1.3)
yellowish (1.6P)
yes (1.1)
yet (2.4P)
you (1.1)
young (1.3)
your (1.R1)
yours (1.R1)
youth (2.4)

Z

zero (1.1)
zinc (1.10P)
zoo (1.3P)

List of proper names in Pupil's Books 1 and 2

LIST OF PLACE NAMES IN PUPIL'S BOOK 1

A
Acropolis (The)
Andes (The)
Angel Falls (The)
Appenines (The)
Arcadia (The)
Argentina
Arizona
Atlantic Ocean (The)
Australia

B
Battersea
Belgravia
Bermuda
Bexley
Big Ben
Bombay
Botswana
British Museum (The)
Broadway
Buenos Aires

C
Cairngorms (The)
Cambria
Caldong
Canada
Canberra
Caracas
Cardiff
Carlsbad Caverns (The)
Central Park
Chicago
Cleveland
Collosseum (The)
Copacabana Beach
Croydon

D
Dallas
Detroit
Dublin

E
Eiffel Tower (The)
England

F
Fifth Avenue
France

G
Gardenia (The)
Glasgow
Golden Gate Bridge (The)
Grand Canyon (The)
Great Russell Street
Greece
Greenland

H
Hamburg
Hampstead
Hampton
Harlem
Henley
Highway (The)
Hollywood Studios
Holton
Houses of Parliament (The)
Houston

I
India
Ireland
Islington
Italy

K
Kalahari Desert (The)
Kosciusko
Kremlin (The)
Kyoto

L
Lambeth
London
Los Angeles
Louvre (The)

M
Malden
Malden Drive
Manchester

Manhattan Island
Mecca
Melbourne
Mercia
Metropolitan Museum (The)
Mexico City
Miami
Midwest (The)
Montreal
Morwell Street
Murray Street

N
National Gallery (The)
New Orleans
New South Wales
New York
New Zealand
North Mimms
Notting Hill

O
Osaka
Oxford

P
Paris
Phoenix
Pink House (The)
Polar areas
Prado Museum (The)

R
Richmond
Rio de Janeiro
Ritting
Ritz (The)
Rockies (The)
Rome
Rose (The)
Royalty (The)

S
Scotland
Siberia
Snowy Mountains (The)
Somerset Road

South America
Southern Angola
St Louis
Statue of Liberty (The)
Sugar Loaf Mountain (The)
Superdome (The)
Sydney

T
Taj Mahal (The)
Texas
River Thames (The)
Tivoli Gardens (The)
Tower Hill
Tower of Pisa (The)
Trafalgar Square
Twin Cities (The)

U
United Kingdom (The)
Urals (The)

V
Vancouver

W
Wales
Wall Street
Washington
White House (The)
Wimbledon

LIST OF PEOPLE'S NAMES IN PUPIL'S BOOK 1

A
Mr Anderson
Anne

B
Mr Baker
Mr Black
Brenda
Mr Brooke
Mr Brown
Mr Burton

C
Caroline
Christopher
Mr Clark
Mr Cliffe
Colombus
Mr Collins
Mr Crocker

F
Mr Fisher
Frank
Fred
Frederick

G
George
Gloria
Mr Gould
Mr Grant
Mr Green

H
Mr Harris
Mr Harrison
Harvey
Helen
Mr Holt

J
Jack
James
Jennifer
Jim
John
Mr Jones

K
Kate

L
Mr Landy
Mr Lewis

M
Mr Macdonald
Mabel
Madeleine
Mr Maitland
Marion
Mary
Mary Lou
May
Michael

N
Nat

O
Otis

P
Mr Parker
Mr Parson
Peter

R
Rodney

S
Sally
Sheila
Mr Sinclair
Mr Smethurst
Mr Smith
Susan

T
Mr Taylor
Tom

W
Mr Watson
Mr West
Mr White
Mr Wilkins
William Pitt

LIST OF PLACE NAMES IN PUPIL'S BOOK 2

A
Alabama
Algmeda
Ambleside
America
Amsterdam
Apollinaris Springs
Arizona
Ashington
Ashmolean Museum (The)
Australia
Avon Valley (The)

B
Barcelona
Beaumont Street
Belgium
Birdcage Walk
Birmingham
Bookham
Bordeaux
Boston
Bradford
Brazil
Brentford
Brigham City
Bristol
Britain
Broad Street
Broughton Tower

Brussels
Buckingham Palace
Burford

C
Calais
California
Canada
Cardiff
Castle Street
Catte Street
Cheshire
Cheyenne
Chicago
Clarendon Hill
Cody
Colorado
Columbia
Coniston Water
Connecticut
Cornmarket Street
Corsica
Cotswolds (The)
Cromwell Hill
Croydon
Cuba

D
Dakotas
Detroit
Dover
Dray Valley (The)
Duddon Bridge

E
Ecuador
Edinburgh
Egypt
Eiffel Tower (The)
El Salvador
England
(Lake) Erie
Esk Valley (The)

F
Fingleton Forest
Finland
Fleet Street
Florida
Florence
France

G
Geneva
Genoa
George Street
Georgia

German
Glasgow
Grand Canyon (The)
Grasmere
Grassington
Gravestone
Greece
Grizedale Forest
Guatemala
Guildhall (The)

H
Hamilton
Hampton
Hard Knott Pass
Helsinki
Hepton
High Street
Holland
Holywell Street
(Lake) Huron

I
Idaho
Illinois
Indiana
Ireland
Italy

J
Jamaica
Japan

K
Kansas
Kendal
Kentucky
Kingston
Kinshasa

L
Las Vegas
Law Courts (The)
Leeds Road
Little Clarendon Street
Liverpool
Livingstone
London
Longwall Street
Louisiana
Louisville
Ludgate Hill

M
Madrid
Magdalen Street
Maine

Mall (The)
Mammoth Hot Springs
Manaos
Manchester
Mansfield Road
Market Street
Massachussetts
Melbourne
Merton Street
Mexico
Miami
Michigan
Minnesota
Mississippi (The)
Monk Lake
Montana
Montreal
Moreton
Mozambique
Muncaster
Munich

N
Naples
Nayarit
Nebraska
Nelson's Column
Nepal
New Orleans
New York
New Zealand
Nice
Nigeria
Norway
Nottingham

O
Oxford

P
Panama
Parks Road
Paris
Peru
Philippines (The)
Pudding Lane

Q
Queen Street

R
Radcliffe (The)
Reigate
Richmond
Rio
Rome
Rose Avenue

S
Salt Lake City
San Francisco
Sardinia
Scotland
(Mt) Sheridon
Shipley
Shoshore Lake
Sicily
South Parks Road
Spain
Speedwell Street
St. Aldates
St. Cross Road
St. Clement Dane's Church
St. Giles
St. Paul's Cathedral
Strand (The)
Stratford
Superdome (The)
(Lake) Superior
Surrey
Switzerland

T
Texas
Thames Street
Tokyo
Toronto
Tower Bridge
Trafalgar Square
Turl Street

U
Ure Valley (The)
USA (The)
Utah

V
Vancouver
Venezuela
Venice
Vietnam
Virginia

W
Walton Street
Warwick
(Mt.) Washbourne
Washington
Waterloo Station
Westgate Shopping Centre
Westminster Abbey
Winchester
Windermere
Windsor
Wisconsin

Woodstock Road
Wyoming

Y
Yellowstone Park
York Crescent
Yorkshire
Yugoslavia

Z
Zaire

LIST OF PEOPLE'S NAMES IN PUPIL'S BOOK 2

A
Alan
Albert
Alcock
Aldrin
Alice
Anne
Armstrong
Arthur

B
Bachs (The)
Baird
Balboa
Bell
Bert
Bill
Billy
(Mr) Black
(Mr) Blake
Bob
(Mr) Bond
(Mr) Brown

C
Cabral
Carol
Cassius Clay
Charles Chaplin
Christian Barnard
Christopher Wren
(Mr) Church
(Mr) Clark
Columbus
(Mr) Cook
(Mr) Croft

D
(Mr) Dale
Diane

Dinsdale
Doug

E
Edmund Hillary
Elaine

F
(Mr) Fielding
(Mr) Finch
Fiona
Floyd Patterson
Frank
Fred
(Mr) Fry

G
George Foreman
(Mr) Green
(Mr) Grimes
Gutenberg

H
Harry
Hartog
Helen
Henry
Hilda

J
Jack
James
Jane
Jantzen
Jean
Jill
Jim
Joe Frazier
John Hunt
(Mr) Jones

K
Karen
(Mr) Kirby

L
(Mr) Laker
Leon Spinks
Linda
Liz
Lorena
Luther

M
Mabel
Machiavelli
Madeleine

Magellan
Marconi
Marion
Mary
Mary Lou
(Mr) Mason
Mata Hari
Michelangelo
Mike
(Mr) Mole
Munro-Morris

N
Nat
Nobel

O
Orville Wright

P
Pat
Paul Gauguin
Pauline
Peter
(Mr) Phillips
Pizarro

(Mr) Powell
(Mr) Power

R
(Mr) Ramsbottom
(Mr) Roach
Roald Amundsen
(Mr) Robinson
Ronald

S
Sally
(Mr) Scott
Sharon
(Mr) Sharp
Sheila
(Mr) Simmons
(Mr) Small
(Mr) Smith
(Mr) Snell
Sonny Liston
(Mr) Starr
Stephen
(Mr) Stewart
(Mr) Stone
Sue

Susan

T
Ted
(Mr) Temple
Tensing
Tony
Tracey

V
Valerie
Vasco Da Gama
Vivian

W
Walter
(Mr) Watson
Wendy
(Mr) West
Wilbur Wright
(Mr) Wilkins
William

Y
Yuri Gagarin
Yvonne